Applying Statistics in Institutional Research

Bernard D. Yancey, *Editor*
University of Colorado, Boulder

NEW DIRECTIONS FOR INSTITUTIONAL RESEARCH

PATRICK T. TERENZINI, *Editor-in-Chief*
University of Georgia

MARVIN W. PETERSON, *Associate Editor*
University of Michigan

Number 58, Summer 1988

Paperback sourcebooks in
The Jossey-Bass Higher Education Series

Jossey-Bass Inc., Publishers
San Francisco • London

Bernard D. Yancey (ed.).
Applying Statistics in Institutional Research.
New Directions for Institutional Research, no. 58.
Volume XV, Number 2.
San Francisco: Jossey-Bass, 1988.

New Directions for Institutional Research
Patrick T. Terenzini, *Editor-in-Chief*
Marvin W. Peterson, *Associate Editor*

New Directions for Institutional Research is published quarterly by
Jossey-Bass Inc., Publishers (publication number USPS 098-830), and
is sponsored by the Association for Institutional Research. The volume
and issue numbers above are included for the convenience of libraries.
Second-class postage paid at San Francisco, California, and at
additional mailing offices. POSTMASTER: Send address changes
to Jossey-Bass Inc., Publishers, 350 Sansome Street, San Francisco,
California 94104.

Editorial correspondence should be sent to the Editor-in-Chief,
Patrick T. Terenzini, Institute of Higher Education, University of
Georgia, Athens, Georgia 30602.

Library of Congress Catalog Card Number LC 85-645339

International Standard Serial Number ISSN 0271-0579

International Standard Book Number ISBN 1-55542-921-1

Cover art by WILLI BAUM

Manufactured in the United States of America. Printed on acid-free paper.

Ordering Information

The paperback sourcebooks listed below are published quarterly and can be ordered either by subscription or single copy.

Subscriptions cost $48.00 per year for institutions, agencies, and libraries. Individuals can subscribe at the special rate of $36.00 per year *if payment is by personal check.* (Note that the full rate of $48.00 applies if payment is by institutional check, even if the subscription is designated for an individual.) Standing orders are accepted.

Single copies are available at $11.95 when payment accompanies order. (California, New Jersey, New York, and Washington, D.C., residents please include appropriate sales tax.) For billed orders, cost per copy is $11.95 plus postage and handling.

Substantial discounts are offered to organizations and individuals wishing to purchase bulk quantities of Jossey-Bass sourcebooks. Please inquire.

Please note that these prices are for the calendar year 1988 and are subject to change without notice. Also, some titles may be out of print and therefore not available for sale.

To ensure correct and prompt delivery, all orders must give either the *name of an individual* or an *official purchase order number.* Please submit your order as follows:

> *Subscriptions:* specify series and year subscription is to begin.
> *Single Copies:* specify sourcebook code (such as, IR1) and first two words of title.

Mail orders for United States and Possessions, Latin America, Canada, Japan, Australia, and New Zealand to:
> Jossey-Bass Inc., Publishers
> 350 Sansome Street
> San Francisco, California 94104

Mail orders for all other parts of the world to:
> Jossey-Bass Limited
> 28 Banner Street
> London EC1Y 8QE

New Directions for Institutional Research Series
Patrick T. Terenzini *Editor-in-Chief*
Marvin W. Peterson, *Associate Editor*

The Association for Institutional Research was created in 1966 to benefit, assist, and advance research leading to improved understanding, planning, and operation of institutions of higher education. Publication policy is set by its Publications Board.

For information about the Association for Institutional Research, write:

AIR Executive Office
314 Stone Building
Florida State University
Tallahassee, FL 32306

(904) 644-4470

Contents

Editor's Notes

The compiling of this volume was motivated by the concern among several members of the profession that there are a number of useful statistical methods not widely known or appreciated. It was also felt that some frequently used methods had become so commonplace that their appropriate and intended uses had become lost in the mythology of the profession and that they were sometimes being applied mechanically without a full understanding of how or when they should be used. The intent of this volume is to provide an overview of some of the more useful statistical methods and to remind the reader that associated with each of these methods are specifically stated underlying assumptions that must be considered in determining when and how to apply them.

Chapter One sets the stage for the following discussions by noting the differences between the research situation often facing the institutional researcher and the circumstances dictated by the classical experimental paradigm. While the classical paradigm assumes complete control over the experimental conditions, such control is seldom seen or exercised by the average institutional researcher.

The second chapter provides a discussion of appropriate statistical methods for comparing groups when the variables to be compared are continuous. The topics discussed cover the t test (both correlated and uncorrelated), ANOVA (analysis of variance), and reminders of the underlying statistical assumptions associated with each of these methods.

Chapter Three seeks to address the problem of what to do with questions that are similar to those covered by the methods discussed in Chapter Two, but for which the data are categorical. This chapter addresses an extremely useful class of statistical methods that has only recently started to gain popularity in the profession, *log-linear models*. The chapter provides an introduction to the methodology for researchers considering the approach, and an excellent review for longtime users.

The topic of Chapter Four is one of the standard statistical methods applied in institutional research, *regression analysis*. Regression analysis has become so commonly used that institutional researchers sometimes tend to forget that the term refers to a class of analysis methods, not to a single method, and that the methodology carries a set of rigid underlying statistical assumptions whose lack of satisfaction can greatly impact the usefulness of the analysis. This chapter provides several examples of the application of the methodology along with a discussion of approaches to determine if the underlying statistical assumptions have been met. In addition, a discussion of influence and multicollinearity is also provided.

1

Chapter Five expands the material presented in Chapter Four toward a more complex situation in which the goal is to examine the relationships among several variables. The methodologies discussed in the chapter, path analysis and its less restrictive maximum likelihood counterpart, LISREL, provide extremely useful approaches when multiple simultaneous relationships among variables need to be investigated or described. This chapter provides an introduction for institutional researchers considering one of these approaches.

The material in Chapter Six concentrates on statistical methods for forecasting. Perhaps because of their statistical complexity, such methods are seldom attempted by institutional researchers. The first part of the chapter provides a perceptive discussion of the various approaches to the problem of forecasting. The remainder of the chapter includes a discussion of one such method, the *Box-Jenkins* forecasting approach, and its application in an institutional research setting, enrollment forecasting. While the level of statistical knowledge and sophistication needed to fully understand the methodology is higher in this chapter than for the other chapters, it is hoped that the methodology's potential, as demonstrated by the example, will encourage readers to spend the extra time needed.

The final chapter describes a class of statistical methods, exploratory data analysis, that can be applied when the primary goal of the analysis is not to test hypotheses, but to gain an understanding of the underlying characteristics of the data. Exploratory data analysis methods can also be used in conjunction with traditional confirmatory analysis methods to determine which of these methods is most appropriate and if the underlying statistical assumptions have been met.

Each of the chapters contains examples taken from an institutional research setting, along with a closing section suggesting available computer software. While this volume cannot comprehensively cover the wide variety of statistical tools available to the institutional researcher, the editor and the contributing authors hope that statistical methods discussed here can at least provide a starting point in the search for an appropriate and useful set of statistical tools.

This volume only scratches the surface of the many statistical methods available to the institutional researcher. I hope the material presented here will stimulate curiosity and interest in learning more about these methods, and that this search will be accomplished with appropriate care and concern for statistical analysis as an art rather than a science. Although statistical analysis provides the institutional researcher with a powerful set of tools to gather information and to aid decision making, its use also carries a great potential for abuse and misuse if applied or interpreted inappropriately. The institutional researcher seeking a cookbook approach for the selection and application of specific statistical methods is doomed to failure and disappointment. The key to successful application of statistical analysis in the institutional research setting lies in the continuous search for the full understanding of how and why the specific methods are derived, the circumstances under which they are appropriately applied, and most important, the continued willingness to question any statistical analysis results that oppose a commonsense notion of the circumstances.

Bernard D. Yancey
Editor

Bernard D. Yancey is director of institutional research for the University of Colorado at Boulder. He has been a practicing institutional researcher for over thirteen years with a keen interest in the relevant application of statistical methods to the problems of institutional research.

Statistical analysis must be approached rationally and with intent, using a systematic plan. The random application of statistical analysis is neither efficient nor likely to produce useful results.

Institutional Research and the Classical Experimental Paradigm

Bernard D. Yancey

For the results obtained from statistical analyses to be most useful and meaningful, the analyses must be carried out in the context of a research design or plan. A research plan is the starting point of any statistical investigation. The plan provides the strategy for addressing the questions that have inspired the study. The importance of the plan cannot be overlooked. Not only does it provide a road map, but by its very nature the plan defines the statistical tools and methods that can be suitably applied, as well as the underlying statistical assumptions that must be met for the analysis results to be meaningful. The widely accepted classical experimental paradigm provides a general framework for such a plan. The initial task facing the institutional researcher is deciding if this paradigm provides the most appropriate strategy for the situation at hand.

The focus of this chapter is on statistical analysis methods, and the terms *research* or *experimental design* are being used in the tradition of Fisher (1925, 1935) and not as used by Campbell and Stanley (1963). The concepts underlying experimental design as discussed here focus on their implications for statistical analysis and statistical methods and not

B. D. Yancey (ed.). *Applying Statistics in Institutional Research.*
New Directions for Institutional Research, no. 58. San Francisco: Jossey-Bass, Summer 1988.

toward appropriate designs for collecting data, the focus of the work by Campbell and Stanley (1963).

From a statistical viewpoint, one of Fisher's most enduring and fundamental contributions is his recognition of the importance and usefulness of randomization as a means of achieving preexperimental equating of groups. Randomization controls external variables in an experimental setting that otherwise might only have been addressed through a laborious matching process.

In the Fisherian sense, the classical experimental paradigm provides a framework for conducting statistical analysis. The question is whether or not this paradigm and its associated variations are in themselves totally sufficient or always most appropriate for the institutional researcher. In addition, if such a paradigm is used, what are the limitations and assumptions associated with the statistical methods?

To address these questions, let us look at the characteristics of the classical experimental paradigm and contrast them to the situation encountered by the institutional researcher.

Classical Experimental Paradigm

Two key elements of the classical experimental paradigm are control, most often obtained by the use of randomization, and the existence of a treatment. Randomization provides a statistical means to equate the groups to be compared and, in particular, to control for variables extraneous to the treatment condition. The importance of randomization cannot be too strongly stressed. Randomization forms the cornerstone of the classical experimental approach and is one of the basic underlying assumptions of the statistical methods applied under such an approach.

Another general characteristic of this approach is that the data to be analyzed are based on a random sample drawn from an infinite population or a finite population with replacement, ensuring that the observations are not only random but also independent. In the absence of a truly infinite population or the ability to sample with replacement, one approach is to follow the suggestion of Fisher (1922) and construct a hypothetical infinite population, considering the actual data a random sample. The specification of this hypothetical infinite population can often be extremely difficult, if not impossible.

The goal of the analysis, however, is usually to gain information not about the sample, but rather about the population from which it is drawn. The problem then becomes one of making inferences about the population based on information gained from the sample. Some formal mechanism for making and testing these inferences is needed; hypothesis testing and statistical significance provide such a mechanism.

Hypothesis testing involves a comparison of observed sample data against a hypothetical or hypothesized population, while significance testing helps determine the possibility that the sample data share the characteristics of the hypothesized population when certain underlying statistical prerequisites are met.

Basic prerequisites must be satisfied before the results of any significance testing can be considered valid: The first and foremost is that the sample must be drawn using a known probability model such as stratified random sampling or, at minimum, drawn as a simple random sample. Even if this is done, note as Morrison and Henkel state: "Significance tests however, are not legitimately used for any purpose other than that of assessing a sampling error of a statistic designed to describe a particular possibility on the basis of a probability sample" (1969, p. 132). Significance tests cannot tell if two groups are different, but rather only the likelihood of obtaining a particular value for a test statistic under certain conditions.

Data Analysis Within the Paradigm. The basic design of the paradigm includes the following sequential steps: (1) developing a question, theory, or hypothesis, (2) determining the research design, (3) collecting the data, (4) analyzing the data, and (5) interpreting the results to determine whether the hypothesis can be supported or should be rejected.

Data analysis within the classical experimental paradigm is closely associated with what might be described as confirmatory data analysis (Tukey, 1980), in which an attempt is made to confirm a hypothesis or theory. This type of data analysis requires careful and meticulous planning and fits quite well within the framework of the experimental paradigm.

The Institutional Research Situation

Now let us look at the institutional researcher's situation. First, the specific steps of the research paradigm that the institutional researcher will follow are often dictated by the questions that have been raised and the characteristics of the data. This contrasts with the experimental paradigm within which the researcher has total control in the design of the study, with the majority of the planning being completed prior to data collection.

Second, the institutional researcher is seldom presented with a data set or a sample either randomly drawn or drawn using a known probability model. In fact, the institutional researcher may not be dealing with a sample at all, but with an entire population. In addition, in some instances the institutional researcher may have had little or no control over the data collection process.

Finally, the primary goal of the research is often different from situations in which the classical experimental paradigm is being applied.

The goal of the institutional researcher is often to gather information that can immediately aid the decision-making process rather than in testing hypotheses. The institutional researcher is frequently confronted with problems that need immediate solutions. This is the case particularly when the researcher's results are to be used directly in the planning process or to determine if a particular program or policy has had the desired impact. Under the classical experimental paradigm, a research study begins with theory, either existing or newly derived. In an institutional research setting, a research study usually begins as a matter of practical expedience. Perhaps a theoretical framework for the study is not even being considered, but if it is, the theoretical framework may be derived only after a good part of the analysis has been performed.

Data Analysis Within the Institutional Research Paradigm. In contrast to the experimental paradigm, there may be no specific sequential steps that can be followed by the institutional researcher. The following, however, might provide a simple example. With one specific set of conditions, the basic steps would be as follows: (1) identify the specific question or problem, (2) design the study, (3) collect the data, (4) analyze the data, (5) determine whether or not the analysis reveals an answer or solution.

If an answer is not revealed at step five, then any or all of steps two through four may be repeated. The analysis described here can be characterized as exploratory data analysis (Tukey, 1980). Predefined hypotheses or theories are not necessarily being tested, but rather, an understanding of the nature and interrelationships in the data is being sought.

Implications for Statistical Analysis

The experimental paradigm provides the researcher with an extremely useful framework for conducting statistical analysis, if the researcher fully understands the basic assumptions that provide the foundation for the paradigm and if the primary purpose of the analysis is confirmatory in nature. If this is not the case, then the classical experimental paradigm may not be appropriate. The use of statistical methods which assume such a paradigm when it does not exist can produce some rather undesirable consequences.

For example, randomization is a statistical approach for equating groups that are to be compared. Randomization provides a means to control extraneous variables that can potentially impact the results of a study, but that are not specifically related to the question at hand. If randomization has not occurred, then these extraneous variables will need to be controlled in another manner.

The impact of sampling strategies and whether or not the analysis is being performed on a sample or on a population can be seen in the following example. In institutional and educational research importance is placed on the power of the central limit theorem that states: The distribution of means, calculated on the basis of repeated random samples of values that are independently and identically distributed, approaches the normal distribution as the number of samples increases. This theorem is often used as an excuse for applying statistical methods that assume normality when the normality assumption cannot be exactly satisfied. A key requirement is that the variables be independently distributed. This is the case only when the sample is being taken from an infinite population or from a finite population with replacement. Observations sampled from a finite population without replacement are not independent, and thus the central limit theorem does not necessarily hold (Lindgren, 1968). The results of any statistical analysis whose derivation is dependent on the central limit theorem may be considered in doubt if the sample was drawn from a finite population without replacement.

On a more basic level, the institutional researcher is often dealing with population data and not samples. In such situations, is significance testing really necessary or even desirable?

Some Final Notes

Without the framework provided by the experimental paradigm, it is doubtful that a large number of statistical methods in common use today would ever have been developed. However, although this paradigm can be extremely useful, reliance on the paradigm carries a set of basic underlying assumptions that must be considered when interpreting the results of any statistical analysis conducted within the paradigm. A failure to satisfy the basic assumptions of randomization and strictly controlled sampling procedures when using the classical experimental paradigm may produce statistical analysis results of questionable validity and quality.

In the typical situation encountered by the institutional researcher, is the classical experimental paradigm and its reliance on confirmatory data analysis always the most appropriate? The complexity of the questions facing the institutional researcher make it likely that a combination of confirmatory and exploratory data analysis approaches, including the application of statistical analysis methods traditionally associated with confirmatory data analysis in an exploratory sense.

The following chapters provide examples of how a variety of appropriate statistical tools can be applied to address a wide range of problems in an institutional research setting, as long as the limitations imposed by the underlying statistical assumptions not only of the methods, but also of the paradigm in which they are implemented are fully

10

understood. The statistical methods discussed cover both confirmatory and exploratory data analysis methods in the context of the classical experimental paradigm when appropriate and in situations that do not necessarily fit the stringent requirement of the paradigm when they cannot be met. The chapters include examples of methods that can be considered useful and appropriate for a variety of problems facing the institutional researcher.

References

Campbell, D. T., and Stanley, J. C. *Experimental and Quasi-Experimental Designs for Research*. Boston: Houghton Mifflin, 1963.

Fisher, R. A. "On the Mathematical Foundations of Theoretical Statistics." *Philosophical Transactions of the Royal Society of London*, Series A, 1922, *222*, 309–368.

Fisher, R. A. *Statistical Methods for Research Workers*. London: Oliver and Boyd, 1925.

Fisher, R. A. *The Design of Experiments*. London: Oliver and Boyd, 1935.

Lindgren, B. W. *Statistical Theory*. New York: MacMillan, 1968.

Morrison, D. E., and Henkel, R. E. "Significance Tests Reconsidered." *The American Sociologist*, 1969, *4* (2), 131–140.

Tukey, J. "We Need Both Exploratory and Confirmatory." *The American Statistician*, 1980, *34* (1), 23–25.

Bernard D. Yancey is director of institutional research for the University of Colorado at Boulder. He has been a practicing institutional researcher for over thirteen years with a keen interest in the relevant application of statistical methods to the problems of institutional research.

It is never safe to use a t or an ANOVA test without first doing some checking. All the methodological and numeric assumptions that underlie the statistic must be met.

Comparing Groups Using Continuous Data

Michael Yost

Individuals involved in institutional research frequently encounter research situations in which they must compare two or more groups of subjects on one variable. In many of these situations, an investigator has had little or no control over study design, sampling procedure, experimental treatment delivery, or data gathering procedures. Often the investigator is given the data at the conclusion of the data gathering portion of the study, told the hypotheses, asked to analyze the data, and expected to assist in the interpretation of the results. If the data in the study are continuous and the sample is of a given size, then the investigator will probably use either a t test or an *analysis of variance* (ANOVA). Frequently, however, use of these statistics is inappropriate because of the conditions under which the data were gathered or the way they were gathered. The purpose of this chapter is to examine the assumptions underlying the t test and ANOVA and to discuss the effects of violations of each assumption on the analyses of data gathered in institutional research settings.

Measurement Scales

Since we are to examine both the t test and ANOVA, we begin by examining the types of data that can be analyzed using these statistical techniques. Data analyzed using either technique should be continuous

B. D. Yancey (ed.). *Applying Statistics in Institutional Research.*
New Directions for Institutional Research, no. 58. San Francisco: Jossey-Bass, Summer 1988.

and meet the specifications of either interval or ratio measurement scales. Both scales assume continuous, equal-interval, mutually exclusive categories of measurement. The interval measurement scale assumes that the data have an arbitrary zero, while the ratio measurement scale assumes an absolute zero. IQ or achievement test scores are examples of interval measures, whereas height, weight, number of dollars budgeted, and number of days spent on a task are examples of ratio measures.

Occasionally, an investigator will attempt to analyze data obtained through the use of a Likert scale (for example: all, some, none, N/A) with a *t* test or ANOVA. With very few exceptions, the data gathered using this type of an instrument fits the specifications of an ordinal measurement scale rather than an interval or ratio measurement scale. Likert scales are subdivided into three to nine intervals, and there is seldom reason to believe that each of the intervals is of the same length. The analysis of Likert scale data using the *t* test or ANOVA therefore may produce questionable results.

The *t* Test

The distinction between large-sample and small-sample statistics is not absolute. If you ask how small N must be before we have a small sample, you will get different answers from different people. General agreement among statisticians is that the division lies in the range of twenty-five to thirty. Small-sample methods may be used regardless of the size of N, but the need for small-sample treatment increases as N decreases, and the need very quickly becomes critical below an N of thirty.

While the *t* test can be used in many different ways for many different purposes (see Veldman and Young, 1981; Mendenhall, 1971), this discussion will be limited to its application to the statistical technique in comparisons where the observations across the groups are correlated and where they are noncorrelated. Several formulas designed for the computation of *t* with noncorrelated samples exist. The formula for a *t* test for the difference between noncorrelated means is

$$t = \frac{M_1 - M_2}{\sqrt{\left(\dfrac{\Sigma x_1^2 + \Sigma x_2^2}{N_1 + N_2 - 2}\right)\left(\dfrac{N_1 + N_2}{N_1 N_2}\right)}}$$

where M_1 and M_2 = means of the two samples

Σx_1^2 and Σx_2^2 = sums of squares in the two samples

N_1 and N_2 = number of cases in the two samples.

Actually, the complete numerator of the equation should read $M_1 - M_2 - 0$ to indicate that it represents a deviation of a difference from the mean of the differences. The entire denominator is the standard error (SE) of the difference between the means.

When considering the difference between means, it is necessary to examine two variations. The first is the variation in the two means that are to be compared, and the second is the variation in the distribution of means in the population from samples of a given size. Means are independently sampled when they are from samples drawn at random from totally different, unrelated groups. In order to test the significance of the difference between two means from a small sample, we use a *t distribution*, which is a mathematical model describing what happens in the case of purely random sampling.

Before examining the exceptions to use of this formula, we should examine an example of its appropriate use. Suppose the communications department in a small private institution wanted to evaluate the effectiveness of two different instructional programs. Both programs are designed to develop students' ability to communicate effectively; that is, the two programs have the same objective. The faculty members in the department were divided over which program was most effective, so they decided to test the null hypothesis that, at the conclusion of the freshman year, there would be no significant difference in the communication ability of the students in the two programs. At the beginning of a school year, fifty-six new freshman communications majors were selected for a study to test the faculty's hypothesis. Prior to the students' arrival on campus, their names were randomly divided into two groups of approximately equal size, and the groups were preregistered into the two classes of the same size (treatment groups). Assume that each student had an equal probability of being placed in either of the groups and that each of the groups had an equal opportunity to receive either of the treatments. The processes of assigning students to groups and assigning the groups to treatments met the assumptions of randomness and independence. One applicant for admission failed to enroll, so one of the classes had one more student.

At the conclusion of the year, all of the students completed the same communications assessment instrument. This instrument had previously been shown to be valid and reliable, and it yielded a score that had the characteristics of an interval measurement scale. The results of the study are listed in Table 1.

With these statistics and the hypothetically ideal experimental design and experimental teaching/working environment, the null hypothesis should be rejected. From the data and the statistics, the faculty inferred that the students in the second instructional program had significantly better communication skills than did the students in the first group.

Table 1. Comparison of Two Independent Groups

	Treatment	
	First	Second
Mean Score	25.4	30.6
Standard Deviation	5.4	5.8
N	27	28

$t = 3.10$

$P < .01$

While the t test is relatively easy to calculate and straightforward to use, there are some situations in which it should be used cautiously and others in which it should not be used at all. In the preceding example, the population from which the fifty-six students were drawn was normally distributed with regard to their communication skills. If the population was not normally distributed, but was seriously skewed, then the results of the t test could have been invalid and misleading. Under these circumstances other statistical tests could have been used. For examples of such tests, including the Wilcoxon rank-sum test, the Kruskal-Wallis test, and tests suggested by Friedman, Cochran, Tukey, and McNemar, the reader is referred to Lehmann (1975).

The t distribution applies only when the sampling has been random. In the example, the sampling met the requirements of randomness, a necessity for a chance-generated mathematical model such as the t distribution. The mathematics of the situation is exact only when sampling is random. Any condition that interferes with randomness of selection of observations makes the estimation of the standard errors and their application in drawing conclusions inaccurate and misleading. If, in the example, the person responsible for the random selection of the students had arbitrarily assigned students to one of the groups or had placed one student in one group because of academic history, then the application of the t statistic would have been questionable.

Random sampling also implies independence of observations (test scores). In the example, the observations were independent because the assignment of one person to a treatment group was not dependent upon the assignment of any other person. To assign one person to a treatment group because a roommate or a friend had been given a previous assignment would have been inappropriate. Other applications to the t distribution take into account the correlation of observations.

The standard deviations of the two samples in the example were similar in magnitude. If the standard deviations of the two samples had been markedly different, then the use of the t test would have been questionable. Whether the two variances are significantly different can be tested with an *F* test. Directions for performing this test can be found in most statistics texts.

Finally, in the example there was a difference in the number of subjects in each of the samples. The *t* test can tolerate some difference in the sample size, providing the samples are not inordinately small. However, when samples become very small with large differences (when one sample is two or three times the size of the other), the results of the *t* test become questionable.

Correlated *t* Tests

In some small-sample institutional research studies, sampling is restricted by matching. The experimental and control groups are often equated in some respect while the effect on some other variable is studied. Groups are frequently equated by matching such variables as age, IQ, socioeconomic level, or the initial score on some particular task or test. It is worthwhile matching samples only on variables that are correlated with the measured outcome—the variable on which we evaluate the experimental outcome. The matching may be for pairs of subjects (for every subject in the control group there is a matching subject in the experimental group) or the subjects in the one group can act as their own control group (each subject has the equivalent of a pre and post measure on the same variable).

The general form of the equation to conduct this type of a *t* test is

$$t = \frac{M_d}{\sigma_m}$$

Where: M_d = the mean of the *N* differences of paired observations
σ_m = the standard error of a mean corrected for the effects of matching.

The number of degrees of freedom for this equation is $N - 1$ where N = the number of pairs of observations.

It follows logically that if we attempt to keep two samples constant with regard to the mean on some variable positively correlated with the experimental variable, the means on the latter will also be kept more constant. The amount of reduction in the variability in the experimental variable will be largely dependent upon the correlation between the control variable and the experimental variable. The standard error of the mean tends to be smaller under this restriction. The general formula for the standard error of the mean of two groups of matched subjects is

$$\sigma_m = \sigma \frac{\sqrt{1 - r_{mx}^2}}{\sqrt{N - 1}}$$

Where σ_m = the standard deviation of the differences in the matched pairs of scores.

r_{mx} = the correlation between the matching variable and the experimental variable.

Although the traditional formula for the standard error of the mean is $\sigma/\sqrt{(N - 1)}$, this formula also includes the factor $\sqrt{(1 - r_{mx}^2)}$. This factor modifies downward the size of the standard error. The larger r becomes, the greater the correction effect. The correlation must be as high as .866 in order to make the size of the correction as much as .50, in which case the standard error is half as large as it would be without matching. The same change in the standard error of the mean could be accomplished by quadrupling the size of the sample without matching samples.

If the matching is done on more than one variable, then the multiple correlation between the experimental variable and the control variables should be used. When there is a single group of subjects on which two correlated measures are obtained, then a different correlation coefficient should be used. In these instances the r value is the test-retest reliability of the measurements on the experimental variables. This value is sometimes called the standard error of the measurement of individuals.

The assumptions underlying the derivation and use of the correlated t test are very similar to those associated with the independent t test. Since the calculation of this statistic involves developing the variance of the difference in pairs of scores, the assumptions associated with the variance of the two groups' not being significantly different and the differences in the N's not being large (when the samples tend to become small) do not apply to the use of this statistic. However, the assumptions of random and independent sampling and the normality of the distribution of the population do apply.

Analysis of Variance

The main differences in the use of the t test and ANOVA is in the size of the samples and the number of comparison groups that each will accommodate. Whereas the t test was designed primarily to analyze small samples, ANOVA was designed for use with both large and small samples. From an experimental design point of view, the t test is designed to analyze data from two groups, whereas ANOVA is designed to compare data for two or more groups. Often used in institutional research, ANOVA is clearly a more complex and versatile statistical analysis tool than the t test.

In institutional research we frequently obtain more than two sets of measurements on the same experimental variable, each under its own set of conditions. The question is whether there are significant differences among the sets. We could, of course, take two sets at a time, pair each one with every other one, and test the significance or the difference between means in each pair. If we tested each pair separately, we would use as an estimate of the population variance only the data from the two samples involved. If we make the null hypothesis apply to all the samples—that they arose by random sampling from the same population—we could use all the data and make a much more stable estimate of the population variance. We would have to assume, of course, that the variances from the different samples are homogeneous. The basic principle of ANOVA is to determine whether the sample means vary further from the population mean than we would expect by chance, in view of the variations of single cases from the same mean. A significant F indicates there are larger variations among the sets of means than expected by chance alone.

Many statistical textbooks describe the varied types of ANOVAs and their use in educational settings (see, for example, Ferguson, 1976; Kerlinger and Pedhazur, 1973; Mendenhall, 1971). Instead of repeating that body of work here, let us examine the assumptions and limitations in the application of the statistic.

There are four assumptions on which ANOVA rests. The first is that the sampling within sets or groups is random; that is, the observations (measurements) are mutually independent and with equal opportunity to occur. When this assumption is completely ignored, the statistic is highly unreliable and questionable. When the groups of subjects are not randomly and independently selected, but the selection and the assignment of subjects to a treatment group are not done using a predetermined bias, then the statistic would be viewed as being reasonably reliable and usable.

The second assumption is that the variances of the scores/measures from within the various sets (groups) must be approximately equal. Much variation among the sets of variances leads to suspicious accuracy of the estimate of the population variance from within the sets.

The third assumption is that the observations within a set should be from normally distributed populations. An F ratio is really only a ratio of two chi squares divided by their respective degrees of freedom, and chi square requires normally distributed populations.

Although these are real assumptions underlying the use of ANOVA, they can be violated somewhat without seriously reducing the reliability of the statistic. In reality, F is rather insensitive to variations in the shape of the population distribution. This is consistent with the known principle that distributions of means (sampling distributions) approach normality even when the populations from which they are drawn may not be normally distributed, providing the variables are randomly drawn and independently distributed. Also, although F is somewhat sensitive to differences in variances of populations, only marked differences in variances have a serious effect on the statistic. As a guide, users of ANOVA should be willing to use the statistic when differences in group variances are small, but not when these differences are large.

The fourth assumption is that the contributions to the total variance must be additive; that is, the total variance is a simple sum of the variances of the groups. This assumption is tied to the first assumption.

Generally, the use of ANOVA assumes that the N for each cell in the analysis contains thirty or more subjects. For example, in a one-factor, three-level statistical analysis there should be ninety or more subjects. Similarly, in a two-factor statistical design with three levels in the first factor and two in the second, a minimum of 180 subjects is necessary. An investigator with a large enough sample and sufficient interest can perform ANOVAs having two, three, or even more factors. However, investigators should be cautious about statistical designs that dilute (subdivide) their sample to the level when one or more of the cells contain too few subjects.

ANOVA, like the t test, can be used with both independent and correlated observations. In the previous explanation about ANOVA, it has been assumed that the observations in any one of the cells are independent of the observations in the other cells. In the two-factor (three-by-two) statistical design described earlier, the 180 subjects would have been included, and there would have been only one measure or score for each of the subjects. In a partially correlated ANOVA design, this study might have been conducted somewhat differently. Assume there were thirty subjects in each of the three levels of the first factor, and a measure or score was obtained on each of these subjects under each of the two experimental conditions (the second factor). This means the observations of the three levels of the first factor are independent, but the observations of the two levels of the second factor are correlated. ANOVA is a very flexible and powerful statistical technique that permits institutional researchers to conduct this type of analysis, as well as analyses that are much more complex.

Whether the analyses are conducted using a yellow tablet and a pencil or a large, complex computer, institutional researchers should use the type or form of ANOVA consistent with the overall design of the experiment. Although computer programs facilitate the ways that data analyses are conducted, many contain documentation that is difficult to understand. If there is any doubt that one has correctly set the analysis parameters on a computer to match the design of the study, first analyze some sample data with known characteristics. Then compare the results of the analysis to the known characteristics of the sample data to ensure that the program is performing the intended analysis.

Repeated Statistical Tests

One of the temptations encountered by institutional researchers using t tests and ANOVAs involves applying multiple tests, essentially repeatedly testing the same variance. Such an approach can have undesirable consequences. For discussion purposes, assume there were two groups of thirty subjects and the experimental design within which data were gathered met all of the assumptions of a t test and ANOVA. As part of the study, each subject completed one of two treatments and two test instruments. The first instrument was an achievement test and the second was an aptitude test. The Pearson correlation between the two measures was found to be .5. By squaring this value and multiplying by 100, approximately 25 percent of the variance of what the achievement instrument tests was also being tested by the aptitude test. Subjects with high achievement tended to have high aptitude, and subjects with low achievement tended to have low aptitude. This relationship has been known for many years.

Now suppose we did an ANOVA using the achievement test data and found that the achievement of one of the groups was significantly higher $(P < .01)$ than the other. From this statistic and our knowledge of the experimental design, we tentatively concluded that one instructional program was more effective than the other. We then conducted another ANOVA using the same procedures used above, except this time we used the aptitude test data. Again we obtained a probability less than .01.

Since the achievement test measured many of the same traits as the aptitude test, was it appropriate to perform the second ANOVA? Was the second statistical test independent of the first? Was the second probability value accurate? Should this be a standard way of applying these procedures in institutional research? The obvious answer to all of these questions is no. Since the tests were correlated, the achievement instrument tested a part of the same variance as the aptitude test. Consequently, the two statistical tests also tested for differences using the same variance. As a result the two statistical tests were not independent, the probability statements were not independent, and the second ANOVA was inappropriate. Statistical tests that can be used in circumstances like those described in this sample problem are covered in detail in statistical textbooks. Investigators involved in institutional research should be careful when they choose the analysis technique that matches the design of the study.

Significant Versus Meaningful Differences

When ANOVA is applied to very large samples (150 or more) of subjects per treatment group, statistically significant differences among the means of the groups of subjects are possible, but are not large enough to be substantially meaningful to an institution. For example, suppose we had a simple two-treatment group experimental design with 200 subjects in one group and 210 in the other. Let us further assume that these independent groups underwent different treatments. At the conclusion of the study one measure was obtained on each subject. The means and standard deviations for Group A were 35.0 and 5.3 and for Group B were 37.2 and 5.8. With these values, it was possible to obtain a probability of less than .05.

Although the probability statement indicates a statistically significant difference in the effectiveness of the treatments, does the difference in the mean scores justify the effort and cost that went into the implementation of the program? When this type of result is obtained, the final decision is usually an administrative or political one and not a statistical one.

Performing the Calculations

Although many statistics textbooks have detailed descriptions of equations to perform t tests and ANOVAs, very few individuals in institutional research actually do the calculations by hand. With the development and proliferation of computers and software, most individuals use computers for their statistical tests.

Using a computer to do a t test or ANOVA demands answers on which statistical package and which computer to use: a personal computer (PC) or a mainframe. Use of a mainframe or a PC is typically a function of computer and software availability and size of the sample. Most investigators of institutional research have access to a PC, but not all have access to a mainframe. For the limited number of subjects usually involved in a study when a t test is used, a PC is the most desirable computer. Because ANOVAs frequently use large samples and require more complex calculations, a mainframe computer tends to be more desirable. Of course, the programs available for each computer and the access to each type of computer influence the final choice of computer.

The debate over which statistical package to use usually centers around availability, cost, ease of use, and whether a particular package will handle a given type of statistical design.

The two most widely used and distributed statistical packages for mainframe computers are the Statistical Package for the Social Sciences (SPSS) and the Statistical Analysis System (SAS). Either program will conduct almost any type of t test or ANOVA that an institutional researcher might need to perform. Both programs are currently available for use on PCs, but users should be aware that both require 512k or more of memory and use more than three megabytes of hard disk space to store programs. Compared with other computer programs on PCs, these programs are relatively expensive. In the category of less expensive and more simplistic programs are StatPac (a registered trademark of Walonick Associates, 6500 Nicollet Ave., Minneapolis, Minn. 55423) and Microstat (a registered trademark of Ecosoft, Inc., 6413 N. College Ave., Indianapolis, Ind. 46220). Both programs will do the calculations for a number of different types of t tests and ANOVAs with very user-friendly characteristics.

Summary

In some areas of their work, institutional researchers are concerned about the accuracy of a statistic and the knowledge that the underlying assumptions have been met. In other areas, they are more interested in the overall value or cost effectiveness of a program. For example, if an investigator was working on a response to an Equal Employment Opportunity Commission (EEOC) charge about hiring or promotions, the accuracy of the statistic would be very important. EEOC offices and many other federal and state offices place much emphasis on the precision of statistics. On the other hand, if an investigator was interested in an evaluation of a new education program, then the accuracy of a statistic becomes less important and the degree to which the program met its intended outcomes or goals becomes more important. Institutional research requires balance and judgment in the use of statistics.

The assumptions on which the t test and ANOVA have been built are almost identical. In the vast majority of institutional research environments, the investigator has limited control over the experimental design of studies. The investigator frequently must recognize that one or more basic assumptions will inevitably be violated; as a result, the investigator works not to eliminate the violations but to reduce the degree to which the assumptions are violated. When the data gathering is completed and the statistical analyses is performed, the analyst must recognize that the final product is not perfect. Instead, the results of the statistical analyses are only an approximate description—sometimes close and sometimes distant—of what really took place in the study. Obviously, the results of statistical analyses in this type of institutional environment should be interpreted very cautiously.

22

References

Ferguson, G. A. *Statistical Analysis in Psychology and Education.* (4th ed.) New York: McGraw-Hill, 1976.

Kerlinger, F. N., and Pedhazur, E. J. *Multiple Regression in Behavioral Research.* New York: Holt, Rinehart & Winston, 1973.

Lehmann, E. L. *Nonparametrics: Statistical Methods Based on Ranks.* San Francisco: Holden-Day, 1975.

Mendenhall, W. *Introduction to Probability and Statistics.* (3rd ed.) Belmont, Calif.: Wadsworth, 1971.

Veldman, D. J., and Young, R. K. *Introductory Statistics for the Behavioral Sciences.* (4th ed.) New York: Holt, Rinehart & Winston, 1981.

Michael Yost is the assistant to the president and director of institutional research at Trinity University in San Antonio, Texas. In the field of institutional research, he has worked on statistical applications, computer modeling, database development, and institutional effectiveness. In the field of neuropsychological research, he has worked on developing and applying statistical analysis techniques.

The data collected in higher education research are not always quantitative or continuous. Until recently, the statistical methods available for analyzing associations among more than two categorical variables were extremely limited.

Using Log-Linear Models in Higher Education Research

Dennis E. Hinkle, Gerald W. McLaughlin, James T. Austin

Data collected and analyzed in higher education research are often qualitative or categorical rather than quantitative or continuous. Examples of qualitative variables are academic discipline, institution type, faculty rank, race, and gender. Until recently, the statistical procedures available for analyzing data of this type were limited. While procedures have long been available for analyzing the association between two categorical variables in a two-dimensional table using chi square statistics, procedures have not been available for analyzing the association among multiple variables in multidimensional, cross-classification tables. For such tables, the usual approach was to analyze various combinations of variables in two-dimensional tables by sequentially combining the levels of the other variables or to analyze two-dimensional tables within the levels of other variables. Such an approach is subject to high Type I error rates; more important, it does not allow the researcher to explore higher-order associations among the variables (Fienberg, 1980).

In the mid to late 1960s social scientists, along with statisticians, began to develop statistical techniques for simultaneous analysis of qualitative or categorical variables in multidimensional contingency tables.

B. D. Yancey (ed.). *Applying Statistics in Institutional Research.*
New Directions for Institutional Research, no. 58. San Francisco: Jossey-Bass, Summer 1988.

These techniques have been referred to as *log-linear contingency table analysis, logit analysis,* or more commonly, *log-linear models.* Those primarily responsible for these developments include Birch (1963), Bishop (1969), Bock (1970), Fienberg, (1972), Grizzle, Starmer, and Koch (1969), Grizzle and Williams (1972), Goodman (1963, 1964, 1970, 1971a, 1971b), Haberman (1972), Kastenbaum (1974), and Roy and Kastenbaum (1956). Even with these pioneering efforts, the use of log-linear models was limited until adequate textbooks were written (for example, Bishop, Fienberg, and Holland, 1975; Fienberg, 1980; Goodman, 1978; Kennedy, 1983; Knoke and Burke, 1980) and until user-friendly computer programs were developed, such as BMDP-4F (BMDP, Inc., 1985), SPSSX and SPSSPC (SPSS, Inc., 1986), SAS (SAS Institute, Inc., 1985), and SYSTAT (1986; a registered trademark of SYSTAT, Inc., 1800 Sherman Ave., Evanston, Ill. 60201). In addition, a number of computer programs specifically designed for categorical data analysis have been written in the last fifteen years, including MULTIQUAL (Bock and Yates, 1973), ECTA (Fay and Goodman, 1975), and FREQ (Haberman, 1979).

The historical roots of log-linear models date to Pearson's chi square (χ^2) test of independence (1900) and Yule's cross product ratio (1900). Pearson's χ^2 is defined as follows:

$$\chi^2 = \frac{\Sigma(O - E)^2}{E}$$

where O = the observed frequencies
    E = the expected frequencies

While both Pearson and Yule restrict their work to 2×2 contingency tables, Bartlett (1935) used Yule's cross product ratio to define and interpret second-order (three variable) interactions in $2 \times 2 \times 2$ contingency tables. Concurrent with these developments was Fisher's (1924) work with maximum-likelihood estimation and his development of a chi square statistic, called the *likelihood ratio chi square* (L^2)

$$L^2 = 2\Sigma(O)\ln(O/E).$$

Both the Pearson χ^2 and the Fisher L^2 are distributed as chi square when samples are sufficiently large and are essentially equivalent for very large samples. However, L^2 has more desirable properties (for example, additivity) for analyzing log-linear models and is the goodness of fit statistic most often used. For a more thorough discussion of the development of statistical techniques for analyzing log-linear models, see Killion and Zahn's (1976) historical bibliography.

Association Models Versus Logit Models

There are two types of log-linear models, *association models* and *logit models*. The purpose of association models is to determine the independence or association between variables (Hinkle and McLaughlin, 1984). Kennedy (1983) refers to these models as "symmetrical" because the research question concerns only the presence or absence of an association between two variables, say A and B. For example, suppose a researcher wants to determine the relationship between the socioeconomic status and retention of community college students in transfer programs. The association between these two variables would be investigated for a sample of community college students; the contingency table for the data analysis might look like Table 1. For the data in this 3×2 contingency table, the appropriate analysis would be the test of independence using either L^2 or χ^2.

In contrast, logit models seek to "determine whether subjects who fall in respective categories of one variable [A] differ appreciably in their response to another variable [B]" (Kennedy, 1983, p. 7). Kennedy refers to these models as "asymmetrical" because variable A is considered the independent or explanatory variable and variable B is the dependent or logit variable. For example, suppose a researcher selects samples of full professors, associate professors, and assistant professors and wants to determine if these three groups differ in their responses to a questionnaire item relating to perceived faculty stress in higher education. The 2×3 contingency table for this investigation might look like that in Table 2. Note that the contingency tables in Table 1 and Table 2 are similar; however, the analysis of the data for Table 2 would be the test of homogeneity rather than the test of independence. Although the actual arithmetic of the chi square tests (either L^2 or χ^2) for Table 1 and Table 2 is the same, the post hoc procedures and the interpretation of the results differ substantially (Marascuilo and McSweeney, 1977). For the association model of Table 1, one suggested post hoc procedure is to compute Cramer's V, a measure of association that can be interpreted in much the same way as a product moment correlation coefficient (Hinkle, Wiersma, and Jurs, 1988). For the logit model of Table 2, the post hoc procedures would be standardized residuals (Hinkle, Wiersma, and Jurs, 1988) or contrasts analogous to Tukey or Scheffe methods (Marascuilo and McSweeney, 1977).

Table 1. Association Model

		Stay	Drop
Socioeconomic	High		
Status	Middle		
	Low		

Hierarchical Log-Linear Models for Multiple Variables

To illustrate the use of hierarchical log-linear models for multiple categorical variables, consider the data discussed by Hinkle and McLaughlin (1984) and found in Table 3. In this example, the researcher was interested in the dropout rates for college students cross classified on the basis of race and gender. While these data best illustrate an example for logit model analysis, we will use them to discuss the association model and then the logit model. For both, we begin by considering a hierarchy of ANOVA-like models, called the log-linear models, and then select the model that is most adequate in explaining the differences in the observed cell frequencies in the $2 \times 2 \times 2$ contingency table. For this three-variable example, one possible hierarchy of models is found in Table 4. The residual and component L^2 statistics computed in the analysis of the association model are also found in this table. We will explain these L^2 values as we illustrate the calculation of the L^2 statistic for the first three models. The calculation of the L^2 statistic for the remaining models is detailed in Fienberg (1980) or Kennedy (1983).

In association model analysis, Model 1 is referred to as the "null model" or the model that would indicate no association among the three variables. For this model, the frequencies would be expected to be uniformly distributed across the eight cells of the $2 \times 2 \times 2$ contingency table; that is, if there is no association among the variables, we would expect each cell to contain $2,859/8 = 357.375$ observations. To test the adequacy of the null model in explaining the distribution of the observed cell frequencies across the cells of the contingency table, Fisher's L^2 statistic is computed. Obviously, the observed cell frequencies are not uniformly distributed across the cells, and we would expect the L^2 statistic to exceed the critical value needed for statistical significance. For the above data, the residual L^2 $(L_1^2) = 2,818.96$, indicating that Model 1 does not adequately fit the observed data. The observed cell frequencies depart appreciably from the frequencies expected with this model.

The next three models sequentially fix the main marginal totals for the three variables. In Model 2, the marginal totals for the variable race (R) are fixed in order to determine whether the distribution of cell frequencies in the $2 \times 2 \times 2$ contingency table can be explained by the fact that there are different numbers of whites and nonwhites in the sample. In this model, the 2,560 white students are uniformly distributed across the other $2 \times 2 = 4$ cells of the contingency table—640 in each cell. Similarly, the 299 nonwhite students are uniformly distributed across the corresponding $2 \times 2 = 4$ cells of the contingency table. The expected frequencies for Model 2 are found in Table 5. The residual L^2 statistic is computed to determine if Model 2 adequately fits the data. Since $L_2^2 = 771.28$, we would conclude that Model 2 does not adequately explain

Table 2. Logit Model

		Full Professor	Associate Professor	Assistant Professor
Response	Agree			
	Disagree			

Table 3. Freshman Retention Data

		Dropout	Stay	Total
White	Male	262	863	1125
	Female	351	1084	1435
Nonwhite	Male	67	77	144
	Female	70	85	155
Total		750	2109	2859

Source: Hinkle and McLaughlin, 1984.

Table 4. Initial Hierarchical Analysis: Models and Likelihood Ratio Chi Square Values

Model		Residual			Component		
		L^2	df	p	L^2	df	p
1	Null	2,818.96	7	.01			
2	R	771.28	6	.01	2,047.68	1	.01
3	R,S	735.16	5	.01	36.12	1	.01
4	R,S,T	62.33	4	.01	672.82	1	.01
5	T,RS	60.426	3	.01	1.91	1	.17
6	RS,RT	0.53	2	.76	59.89	1	.01
7	RS,RT,ST	0.23	1	.63	0.30	1	.58
8	RST	0.00	-	---	0.23	1	.63

the distribution of cell frequencies for the $2 \times 2 \times 2$ contingency table. The component L^2 for this model is the portion of the L^2 attributable to the race variable and is computed by subtracting the residual L^2 for Model 2 from the residual L^2 for Model 1, $L_1^2 - L_2^2 = (2,818.96 - 771.28) = 2,047.68$. Since the L^2 statistics are additive, this single degree of freedom component L^2 statistic indicates that there is an improvement of the fit to the data using Model 2 (that is, there is a difference in the number of white and nonwhites in the sample). However, based upon the residual L_2^2 the fit is still not adequate. We will discuss the component L^2 in more detail in the section concerning model selection.

In the next model in the hierarchy, Model 3, the marginal totals for the variable sex (S) are fixed. In this step, we investigate whether the distribution of cell frequencies in Table 3 can be explained by the fact that there are differences in the number of males (1,269) and females

(1,590) in the sample, having previously controlled for the marginal totals for the variable race (R). For this model, the 1,125 white males are uniformly distributed across the two levels of the variable retention (T). Similarly, the 1,435 white females, the 144 nonwhite males, and the 155 nonwhite females are uniformly distributed across variable T; these expected frequencies are found in Table 6. As for the first two models, the residual L^2 statistic is computed using the observed frequencies of Table 3 and the expected frequencies of Table 6. For this model, the residual L^2 = 735.16, indicating that Model 3 does not adequately fit the data and is not sufficient for explaining the distribution of observed cell frequencies of Table 3. The component L^2 for Model 3 is computed by subtracting L_3^2 from L_2^2: $(L_1^2 - L_2^2)$ (771.28 - 735.16 = 36.12). This component L^2 again indicates a significant improvement in the fit of the data (that is, there is a difference in the number of males and females in the sample), but based upon the residual L^2 for Model 3, the fit is still inadequate. The observed cell frequencies still depart appreciably from the frequencies expected with Model 3.

The final one-variable model in the hierarchy is Model 4. For this model, the marginal totals for the variable retention (T) are fixed. As indicated in the hierarchy, Model 4 is used to investigate whether the difference in the numbers of students who dropped out of school and those who stayed can explain the differences in the observed cell frequencies of Table 3, having previously controlled for the race (R) and sex (S) variables. The calculation of the expected cell frequencies for this model are slightly more complicated and thus are not given; the reader is referred to Fienberg (1980) and Kennedy (1983) for details. However, the residual L^2 for this model (L_4^2 = 62.33) is statistically significant, indicating Model 4 does not fit the data. The component L^2 is 735.16 - 62.34 = 672.82. While this component L^2 indicates a difference in the number

Table 5. Expected Cell Frequencies for Model 2

		Stay	Drop
White	Male	640.0	640.0
	Female	640.0	640.0
Nonwhite	Male	74.75	74.75
	Female	74.75	74.75

Table 6. Expected Cell Frequencies for Model 3

		Stay	Drop
White	Male	562.5	56.25
	Female	717.5	717.5
Nonwhite	Male	72.0	72.0
	Female	77.5	77.5

who stayed, this difference, combined with the differences in the number of whites and nonwhites and the number of males and females, is not sufficient for explaining the distribution of cell frequencies in the $2 \times 2 \times 2$ contingency table (see Table 3).

These first four models do not consider associations among the three variables in this study; they are concerned only with the differences in the marginal frequencies of the variables controlled sequentially. Since none of these models adequately fit the data, one or more of the higher-order log-linear models in the hierarchy are necessary for explaining the distribution of cell frequencies in Table 3. These subsequent models deal sequentially with the three first-order (two-variable) associations (Models 5, 6, and 7) and the one second-order (three-variable) association (Model 8). The sequence of the models in the hierarchy is determined a priori by the researcher. For this example, we chose to examine the race by sex (RS) association—Model 5; the race by retention (RT) association—Model 6; and finally the sex by retention (ST) association—Model 7. However, another researcher might choose another sequence that is substantively justifiable.

The residual L^2 for the race by sex association (RS) ($L_5^2 = 60.42$) is statistically significant, indicating that Model 5 did not fit the data. In addition, the component L^2 ($62.33 - 60.42 = 1.91$) indicates that there is a nonsignificant race by sex association. Now observe Model 6 which considers the race by retention (RT) association; note that the residual L^2 ($L_6^2 = 0.53$) is not statistically significant. This result indicates that the expected cell frequencies, determined by controlling for the marginal totals for the three variables as well as the RS and the RT associations, do not differ from the observed cell frequencies. Note also that the component L^2 ($60.42 - 0.53 = 59.89$) is statistically significant, indicating that the addition of the race by retention (RT) association to the hierarchy is significant in reducing the residual L^2 and also the presence of an RT association. Completing this example, consider Model 7. This model is used to determine whether a sex by retention (ST) association exists after controlling for the other models in the hierarchy. For this model, both the residual L^2 ($L_7^2 = 0.23$) and the component L^2 ($0.53 - 0.23 = 0.30$) are not significant. This was expected since the residual L^2 for Model 6 was already nonsignificant.

Finally, consider Model 8 which is called the "saturated model." The residual L^2 for this model is always zero, since the expected frequencies generated for this model are exactly the same as the observed frequencies. For this example, the component L^2 is also nonsignificant, indicating that less restrictive models in the hierarchy were able to fit the data. If previous models were not able to adequately fit the data, the residual L^2 would still be zero, but the component L^2 would be statistically significant. This result would indicate the presence of a three-variable association; that is, the simple association between two of the variables was not the same over the levels of the third variable.

Strategy for Model Selection

Kennedy (1983) presents a strategy for selecting the most appropriate log-linear model (or models) when the models are considered in a hierarchy. The first step in this strategy is to begin at the bottom of the column of residual L^2 and go up the column looking for the first significant L^2. In our example, the first significant L^2 was for Model 5. This model and all less restricted models (1 through 4) are eliminated from further consideration. The second step is to begin at the bottom of the column of component L^2 and go up the column looking for the first significant component L^2. In the example, the first significant component L^2 was for Model 6. The more restricted models (7 and 8) would also be eliminated from further consideration. Using this strategy, we find that Model 6 would be the model of choice. However, when the associations among more than four or five variables are investigated, this strategy does not always identify a single model. For example, suppose that both the residual L^2 and the component L^2 for Model 6 were statistically significant. Further suppose that the residual L^2 for Model 7 was not significant but that the component L^2 was, as illustrated in Table 7. Using the above strategy, the researcher would possibly eliminate Model 6 and interpret only Model 7. However, results such as those illustrated in Table 7 indicate the presence of both an RT and an ST association.

Non-Hierarchical Log-Linear Analysis

Researchers using the log-linear models in the analysis of qualitative data quickly discover that the default options of the larger, mainframe computer software packages do not automatically provide the residual L^2 and the component L^2 discussed above. The researcher must sequentially enter the models and develop the tables containing both the residual L^2 and the component L^2. However, if the researcher cannot defend the use of a hierarchical approach and is only interested in whether there are one or more first-order (two-variable) associations or a second-order (three-variable) association, a different screening procedure is suggested. This procedure is illustrated in Table 8.

Note that there are two screening tables in Table 8. The first table involves testing whether the k-way or higher order effects are zero; the second table involves the tests of which k-way effects are zero, where k is the number of variables. Consider the first screening table. The test that the "1"-way or higher-order effects are zero is actually the test of Model 1, the null model; the residual $L^2 = 2,818.96$. If this model is not statistically

Table 7. Illustration for Model Selection

	Model	Residual	Component
Null	1	**	
R	2	**	NS
R,S	3	**	NS
R,ST	4	**	NS
T,RS	5	**	NS
RS,RT	6	**	**
RS,RT,ST	7	NS	**
RST	8	NS	NS

Table 8. Screening Tables for Non-Hierarchical Models

A. Tests that K-way and Higher Order Effects are zero

K	L^2	p
1	2818.96	< .0001
2	62.11	< .0001
3	0.23	.6319

B. Tests that K-way Effects are zero

K	L^2	p
1	2756.62	< .0001
2	62.33	< .0001
3	0.23	.6319

significant, we would conclude that the null model adequately fits the data and that there is no association among the variables. However, because this model is statistically significant, the second step would be to look at the test of the "2"-way or higher-order models, which is actually the test of Model 4 ($L^2 = 62.33$). If this test is not significant, we would conclude that the differences in the marginal totals for one or more of the variables can explain the differences in the cell frequencies of the contingency table and that no two-way associations are present. Again, since this L^2 is still significant, we continue the screening procedure and look at the test of the "3"-way or higher-order effect, which is actually the test of Model 7. Note that this L^2 is not statistically significant, indicating that the "3"-way effect (the three-variable association) is zero and that one or more of the two-variable associations are adequate for explaining the distribution of cell frequencies in the contingency table. If the test for $k = 3$ is significant, then the conclusion would be that Model 8, the saturated model, is necessary to fit the data and that a second-order (three-variable) association exists.

In the second screening table of Table 8, the L^2 values are component L^2 rather than residual L^2. These L^2 are computed to test for the significance of families of models. In the first test, the family of single-variable models is considered and tested for statistical significance by subtracting the residual L^2 for Model 4 from the residual L^2 for Model 1: $(L_1{}^2 - L_4{}^2 = 2{,}818.96 - 62.33 = 2{,}756.63)$. If this component L^2 is nonsignificant, then more than just the single-variable models are needed to fit the data and to explain the distribution of observed cell frequencies. However, because this component L^2 is significant, one or more of the single-variable models are significant contributors, and the data would be explored further to determine which of these single-variable models are significant.

The family of two-variable models is considered in the second test of this second screening table. The component L^2 for this second test is determined by subtracting the residual L^2 for Model 7 from the residual L^2 for Model 4: $(L_4{}^2 - L_7{}^2 = 62.33 - 0.23 = 62.10)$. Because this component L^2 is statistically significant, one or more of the two-variable models are significant contributors to the explanation of the distribution of observed cell frequencies. One or more significant first-order (two-variable) associations are present in the contingency table. Subsequent procedures in the following discussion are then used to determine which of these associations are significant.

The final step in the second screening table is the test of the component L^2 for Model 8. As indicated before, this component L^2 $(L_7{}^2 - L_8{}^2 = 0.23 - 0.00 = 0.23)$ was nonsignificant and indicated that less restrictive models were sufficient for explaining the distributions of observed cell frequencies and that a second-order (three-variable) association was not present in the data. As before, if this component L^2 had been significant, the conclusion would have been that Model 8 was necessary for fitting the observed data and that a second-order association existed.

Following these two screening procedures, the process becomes one of determining which of the families of models are required to fit the data. In our example, we determined from the screening procedures that one or more first-order (two-variable) associations are present in the data. In order to determine which ones are present, we recommend looking at the partial L^2 for each of the two-variable models. This process is analogous to examining the partial regression coefficients in multiple regression analysis.

Recall that in multiple regression analysis, each predictor variable is considered after controlling the regression equation for all other variables. In log-linear analysis of association models, each first-order association is considered after controlling for all other first-order associations. The partial L^2 for our example are found in Table 9. Note that only the partial L^2 for the race by retention association (RT) (60.08) is significant. Note also that the sex by retention association (ST) (0.30) is the same as the component L^2 for Model 7 and is nonsignificant. We have also included the partial L^2 for the one-variable models. All three partial L^2 are statistically significant, indicating that there are differences in the

Table 9. Tests of Partial Associations

		L^2	p
Race by Sex	(RS)	2.11	.1463
Race by Retain	(RT)	0.30	.5819
Sex by Retain	(ST)	60.08	<.0001
Race	(R)	2047.68	<.0001
Sex	(S)	36.12	<.0001
Retain	(T)	672.82	<.0001

number of males and females, the number of whites and nonwhites, and the number of students who stay in school and who drop out. Obviously, these latter partial L^2 are of little importance to the researcher except for describing the sample. Thus, based upon the results in Table 9, we would conclude that there is a significant race by retention (RT) association present in the data.

In summary, to this point we have presented two approaches to log-linear analysis for association models. In the first approach, a hierarchical set of log-linear models is developed and tested sequentially. In determining which model or models should be interpreted, a screening strategy using both the residual and component L^2 was discussed. However, if the researcher is unwilling or unable to establish such a hierarchy a priori, a second screening procedure was proposed. The second procedure identifies families of models that are needed to fit the data. Subsequently, partial L^2 statistics are considered to determine which members of the families are contributors to the fit.

Logit Model

Now consider the analysis of the same data using the logit model approach. In this approach, the retention (T) variable is considered as the dependent or logit variable, with race (R) and sex (S) variables considered as the explanatory variables. For this approach, only Models 6, 7, and 8 from Table 4 are models of interest. Are there differences in the retention rates of whites and nonwhites (Model 6-RT)? Are there differences in the retention rates of males and females (Model 7-ST)? Are there differences in the retention rates for the combination of the levels of the race and sex variables (Model 8-RST)? Using ANOVA terminology, Model 6 is the race main effect, Model 7 is the sex main effect, and Model 8 is the race by sex interaction effect.

For the logit model, we can use either a hierarchical approach or a regression (partial L^2) approach; both approaches are illustrated in Table 10. Note that for both approaches, the null model is Model 5, as defined in the association model approach, and contains all three one-variable models and the race by sex (RS) association. If this model adequately fits

Table 10. Logit Model Analysis (Hierarchical)

	L^2	df	p
Enter Race then Sex			
Model			
5　T,RS (Null Model)	60.42	3	< .01
6　RS,RT (Race)	59.89	1	< .01
7　RS,RT,ST (Sex|Race)	0.30	1	.58
8　RST (Race x Sex)	0.23	1	.63
Enter Sex then Race			
Model			
5　T,RS (Null Model)	60.42	3	< .01
6a　RS,ST (Sex)	0.11	1	.74
7a　RS,ST,RT (Race|Sex)	60.08	1	< .01
8　RST (Race x Sex)	0.23	1	.63

the data, then subsequent models, which are the models of interest, are unnecessary for explaining the distribution of observed cell frequencies.

In the hierarchical approach, the order of log-linear models tested is specified by the researcher. In the example, suppose the decision was made to enter race and then sex (see Model 6 in Table 10). This model (RS,RT) is used to determine whether the retention rate is the same for both whites and nonwhites, that is, the race main effect (see Table 10). Model 7 (RS,RT,ST) is then used to determine whether the retention rate is the same for males and females, the sex main effect, after controlling for the race main effect. In the regression (partial L^2) approach, Model 7 (RS,RT,ST) would be used to examine the race main effect after controlling for the sex main effect; Model 7a would examine the sex main effect after controlling for the race main effect. For this example, the race main effect is significant regardless of whether a hierarchical or partial L^2 approach is used, and we would conclude that whites and nonwhites differ in retention rate.

Post Hoc Procedures

The post hoc procedures used in the analysis of simple log-linear models, such as our example, are relatively easy to compute and interpret. In the association model approach, the researcher determines and reports the magnitude of the association between the race (R) and retention (T) variables combined over the sex (S) variable. For this 2×2 contingency table, several measures of association could be used including the phi (ϕ) coefficient (Hinkle, Wiersma, and Jurs, 1988). This $2 \times 2 \times 2$ contingency table along with this measure are found in Table 11. For these data, $\phi = .152$ and is interpreted as a correlation coefficient.

For the logit model, three post hoc procedures can be used: (1) standardized residuals (Hinkle, Wiersma, and Jurs, 1988), (2) Scheffe-type contrasts (Marascuilo and McSweeney, 1977), and (3) tests of the estimates

Table 11. Coefficient for $2 \times 2 \times 2$ Association Model

		Race			
		White	Nonwhite		
Retention	Stay	1947	162	2109	$\phi = .152$
	Dropout	613	137	750	
	Total	2560	299	2859	

of the parameters (Lee, 1977; Kennedy, 1983). We will illustrate the computation of the standardized residuals in interpreting the difference in retention for white and nonwhites. Because the L^2 statistic is computed over all cells of the 2×2 table, a significant L^2 is an omnibus statistic and does not specify which of the cells are the major contributors to the statistical significance. To determine which cells are significant contributors, standardized residuals are computed for each cell using the following formula:

$$\underline{R} = \frac{O - E}{\sqrt{N}}$$

where O is the observed frequency for the cell and E is the expected frequency. The observed frequencies (O), the expected frequencies (E), and the standardized residual (R) for each of the cells of this 2×2 contingency table are found in Table 12. Standardized residuals have been shown to be approximately standard normal (Haberman, 1973). Thus, when an R for a given cell exceeds 2.00 (in absolute value), we would conclude that the cell is a major contributor to the significant L^2 statistic. Further, if the sign of the R is positive, then that cell contains more observed frequencies than expected. Conversely, if the sign is negative, the cell contains fewer observed frequencies than expected. For the example, the standardized residuals in Table 12 indicate that there were fewer than expected whites ($R = -2.260$) and more than expected nonwhites ($R = 6.612$) who dropped out of school and fewer than expected nonwhites ($R = -3.943$) who stayed in school.

Sampling Zeros and Structural Zeros in Log-Linear Analysis

In the previous example, the sample size in the data was quite large. While large sample sizes are not a prerequisite for the analysis of log-linear models, such analyses are subject to the same restrictions as are all chi square analyses, namely, no more than 20 percent of the cells should have expected frequencies (E) less than five, and no cell can have zero entries (Hinkle, Wiersma, and Jurs, 1988). Consider a $2 \times 2 \times 2 \times 3 \times 4$

Table 12. Standardized Residuals for 2 × 2 × 2 Logit Model

| | | Race | | |
		White	Nonwhite	
Retention	O Stay E	1947 1888.37	162 220.63	2109
	O Dropout E	613 671.63	137 78.37	750
Total		2560	299	2859

Standardized Residuals

| | | Race | |
		White	Nonwhite
Retention	Stay	1.347	-3.943
	Dropout	-2.260	6.612

cross-classification table; this table would contain ninety-six cells. For such complex tables, large sample sizes are necessary in order to satisfy the requirement that fewer than 20 percent of the cells have expected frequencies less than five.

Zero cell frequencies can occur for one of two reasons: They can be either *sampling zeros* or *structural zeros*. Sampling zeros occur because the researcher uses a sample rather than the population. For cells in the population that have small frequencies, a cell in the sample could contain no entries even where it is logically possible. For example, it is unlikely to find many grandparents under the age of thirty-five with bachelor's degrees or males over fifty years enrolled in nursing programs at community colleges, even in the largest national samples. In theory, the researcher could remove these zeros by increasing the sample size. Since this approach is often impractical, the researcher must resort to some other solution. One solution is to combine adjacent categories of the variable when it is practical and will not distort the data; however, this approach must be used with caution (Hinkle, Wiersma, and Jurs, 1988). A second approach is to add a small constant, such as .50, to each cell in the contingency table (Goodman, 1970). This method, though used most often, tends to be conservative and underestimates the parameters and their significance (Knoke and Burke, 1980). A third more complex solution is to use maximum-likelihood estimates for the zero cell entries (Fienberg, 1980). While all are viable alternatives, the first two are the simplest to use.

On the other hand, structural zeros arise from combinations that are logical impossibilities, such as male obstetrics patients. The major problem occurs when researchers fail to recognize they have a structural zero rather than a sampling zero and try to remove it using the methods described above. This practice leads to uninformative analyses and must be avoided (Fienberg, 1980). The approaches for dealing with structural zeros are either the analysis of partial tables (Bishop, Fienberg, and Holland, 1975) or the use of quasi-independence models (Goodman, 1968).

Using Log-Linear Models to Test for Discrimination

Log-linear analysis provides a rational procedure for testing the association between gender and various personnel decisions, such as promotion and tenure, which are dichotomous, categorical variables. In these analyses, some writers advocate a search for the best-fitting model (Fienberg, 1980). However, the intent of hypothesis testing is not to let the data dictate the analysis, but to determine if a specified effect is statistically significant. Moreover, if a test procedure considers a large number of alternatives, some of which may be dropped from consideration if nonsignificant, then the nominal significance level is an underestimate of the actual significance level. For example, if twenty effects are tested using the .05 level of significance, then the probability is much greater than .05 that at least one effect will have an apparent significance of .05.

The solution to this dilemma is to develop rules for one specific test of an effect and to compute the probability for that test. In testing for prima facie evidence of discrimination, the first step is to identify the effect that can be uniquely interpreted as evidence of gender-based bias (if there are no other explanations). Note that such a procedure does not prove discrimination: No statistical procedure proves bias. The use of statistics only indicates that the outcomes are related to gender or some other factor in a way not explained by the other elements in the model. Other evidence can then be considered as a basis for the bias.

Table 13. Data for Sex Discrimination Examples

Year	Level	Gender	Decision	
			Yes	No
1984	To.Prof.	Male	25	13
		Female	3	4
	To.Assoc.	Male	44	13
		Female	6	4
1983	To.Prof.	Male	32	18
		Female	1	0
	To.Assoc.	Male	42	17
		Female	10	3
1982	To.Prof.	Male	23	27
		Female	0†	0†
	To.Assoc.	Male	41	11
		Female	7	0‡

† Structural Zero
‡ Sampling Zero

Consider the data in Table 13; the variables investigated are year of consideration (Y), level of promotion (L), and gender (S), with promotion outcome (D) as the logit variable. Note that the cells for females considered for promotion to full professor in 1982 are identified as structural zeros, since no females were considered for this specific personnel action. In addition, there are two cells that are identified as sampling zeros: females not promoted to full professor in 1983 and females not promoted to associate professor in 1982.

In this example, the effect that must be considered as a cause for concern is the interaction of gender and the personnel decision, which indicates that the members of both sexes are not proportionally distributed within the categories of the decision (that is, promotion). Where there are additional measured variables, their interaction with the gender by decision effect must also be considered. The change in the fit of the model with the addition of these elements indicates the statistical significance of possible discrimination interactions. If there is an improvement in fit associated with the inclusion of model with these additional effects, then the exploratory procedures discussed earlier can be used to isolate the source of the significant effect or effects.

The effects that can indicate possible cause for concern are based on the interaction of gender (S) and promotion outcome (D), that is, the SD effect. In this specific example, there are also several higher-order interaction terms that contain the SD effect: its interaction with year (SYD), its interaction with level of promotion (SLD), and its interaction with both year and level of promotion (SYLD). If these terms are dropped from the model, the resulting analysis is based on SLY, LYD, and lower-order terms (for example, LY, SL, SY, YD, LD, A, S, L, Y). Note that none of these terms contain the gender-decision interaction term.

The expected values for the SD model are shown in Table 14. They can be obtained by collapsing across gender, computing the proportion of members receiving the promotion, and multiplying the proportion by the number of each gender. For example, in 1982 there were twenty-nine of forty-seven promoted, so that the proprotion (29/47) when multiplied by the number of males (thirty-nine) gives 24.06 or the 24.1 shown in the table as the expected value for males. This reinforces the notion that this model produces expected values that are independent of a consideration of gender. The residual L^2 for this model (L^2 = 4.18) is nonsignificant. This model does fit the data. Further, the models that include the SD, SYD, SLD, and the SLYD effects will not provide a significantly better fit or prima facie evidence of discrimination. If, however, these latter models were necessary for fitting the data, then the researcher is advised to follow the exploratory strategy of testing models with the sequence dictated by the tests of partial associations (see Table 15). It must also be emphasized that the precision indicated by the print-

Table 14. Expected Frequencies for Sex Discrimination Example

Year	Level	Gender	Decision Yes	No
1984	To.Prof.	Male	24.1	14.9
		Female	4.9	3.1
	To.Assoc.	Male	42.9	15.1
		Female	8.1	2.9
1983	To.Prof.	Male	32.7	18.3
		Female	1.3	0.7
	To.Assoc.	Male	43.0	17.0
		Female	10.0	4.0
1982	To.Prof.	Male	23.5	27.5
		Female	0†	0†
	To.Assoc.	Male	42.6	10.4
		Female	6.4	1.6

† Structural Zero

Table 15. Tests of Partial Associations Sex Discrimination Example

Effect	L^2	p
SLD	0.00	.9666
SYD	3.42	.1800
TYD	3.94	.1393
SLY	3.80	.0512
SD	0.18	.6699
LD	12.34	.0004
YD	0.43	.8074
SL	2.91	.0881
SY	1.32	.5174
LY	0.70	.7061
D	44.24	< .0001
S	185.67	< .0001
L	5.63	.0177
Y	0.53	.7689

out should not be mistaken for accuracy, since each probability level represents the likelihood of a single outcome, not the probability of a large number of alternatives.

Summary

This chapter presents pertinent concepts and procedures for using log-linear and logit analysis in higher education research. In this chapter, we have made the distinction between symmetric and asymmetric designs in both the initial analysis and the post hoc procedures. The examples used in the chapter illustrate the flexibility of the approach in both an analysis of variance and a regression framework. With these data, we hope that the reader will be able to evaluate the strengths and weaknesses of using log-linear models in higher education research.

40

References

Bartlett, M. S. "Contingency Table Interactions." *Journal of the Royal Statistical Society Supplement*, 1935, *2*, 248–252.

Birch, M. W. "Maximum Likelihood in Three-Way Contingency Tables." *Journal of the Royal Statistical Society*, Series B, 1963, *25*, 220–233.

Bishop, Y.M.M. "Full Contingency Tables, Logits, and Split Contingency Tables." *Biometrics*, 1969, *25*, 119–128.

Bishop, Y.M.M., Fienberg, S. E., and Holland, P. W. *Discrete Multivariate Analysis: Theory and Practice*. Cambridge, Mass.: MIT Press, 1975.

BMDP, Inc. *Biomedical Data Programs Statistical Software Manual*. Berkeley: University of California Press, 1985.

Bock, R. D. "Estimating Multinomial Response Relations." In R. C. Bose and others (eds.), *Contributions to Statistics and Probability*. Chapel Hill: University of North Carolina Press, 1970.

Bock, R. D., and Yates, G. *MULTIQUAL, Log-Linear Analysis of Nominal and Ordinal Qualitative Data by the Method of Maximum Likelihood*. Chicago: National Educational Resources, 1973.

Fay, R. E., and Goodman, L. A. *ECTA Program: Description for Users*. Chicago: University of Chicago Press, 1975.

Fienberg, S. E. "The Analysis of Incomplete Multi-Way Contingency Tables." *Biometrics*, 1972, *28*, 177–202.

Fienberg, S. E. *The Analysis of Cross-Classified Categorical Data*. (2nd ed.) Cambridge, Mass.: MIT Press, 1980.

Fisher, R. A. "The Conditions Under Which χ^2 Measures the Discrepancy Between Observed Observation and Hypothesis." *Journal of the Royal Statistical Society*, 1924, *87*, 442–450.

Goodman, L. A. "On Methods for Comparing Contingency Tables." *Journal of the Royal Statistical Society*, Series A, 1963, *126*, 94–108.

Goodman, L. A. "Simultaneous Confidence Limits for Cross-Product Ratios in Contingency Tables." *Journal of the Royal Statistical Society*, Series B, 1964, *26*, 86–102.

Goodman, L. A. "The Analysis of Cross-Classified Data: Independence, Quasi-Independence, and Interaction in Contingency Tables with or Without Missing Cells." *Journal of the American Statistical Association*, 1968, *63*, 1091–1131.

Goodman, L. A. "The Multivariate Analysis of Qualitative Data: Interactions Among Multiple Classifications." *Journal of the American Statistical Association*, 1970, *65*, 226–256.

Goodman, L. A. "The Analysis of Multidimensional Contingency Tables: Stepwise Procedures and Direct Estimation Methods for Building Models for Multiple Classifications." *Technometrics*, 1971a, *13*, 33–61.

Goodman, L. A. "Partitioning of Chi Square, Analysis of Marginal Contingency Tables, and Estimation of Expected Frequencies in Multidimensional Contingency Tables." *Journal of the American Statistical Association*, 1971b, *66*, 339–344.

Goodman, L. A. *Analyzing Qualitative/Categorical Data*. Cambridge, Mass.: Abt Books, 1978.

Grizzle, J. E., Starmer, C. F., and Koch, G. G. "Analysis of Categorical Data by Linear Models." *Biometrics*, 1969, *25*, 489–504.

Grizzle, J. E., and Williams, O. D. "Log-Linear Models and Tests of Independence for Contingency Tables." *Biometrics*, 1972, *28*, 137–156.

Haberman, S. J. "Log-Linear Fit for Contingency Tables (Algorithm AS-51)." *Applied Statistics*, 1972, *21*, 218–225.

Haberman, S. J. "The Analysis of Residuals in Cross-Classified Tables." *Biometrics*, 1973, *29*, 205–220.

Haberman, S. J. *Analysis of Qualitative Data.* Vol. 1. New York: Academic Press, 1979.

Hinkle, D. E., and McLaughlin, G. W. "Selection of Models in Contingency Tables: A Reexamination." *Research in Higher Education*, 1984, *21*, 415–423.

Hinkle, D. E., Wiersma, W., and Jurs, S. E. *Applied Statistics for the Behavioral Sciences.* (2nd ed.) Boston: Houghton Mifflin, 1988.

Kastenbaum, M. "Analysis of Categorized Data: Some Well-Known Analogues and Some New Concepts." *Communications in Statistics*, 1974, *3*, 401–417.

Kennedy, J. J. *Introductory Log-Linear Analysis for Behavioral Researchers.* New York: Praeger, 1983.

Killion, R. A., and Zahn, D. A. "A Bibliography of Contingency Table Literature: 1900–1974." *International Statistical Review*, 1976, *44*, 71–112.

Knoke, D., and Burke, P. J. "Log-Linear Models." *Sage University Paper Series on Quantitative Applications in the Social Sciences*, 07–020. Newbury Park, Calif.: Sage Publications, 1980.

Lee, S. K. "On the Asymptotic Variances of μ Terms in Log-Linear Models of Multidimensional Contingency Tables." *Journal of the American Statistical Association*, 1977, *72*, 412–419.

Marascuilo, L. A., and McSweeney, M. *Nonparametric and Distribution-Free Methods for the Social Sciences.* Monterey, Calif.: Brooks/Cole, 1977.

Pearson, K. "On a Criterion That a Given System of Deviations from the Probable in the Case of a Correlated System of Variables Is Such That It Can Reasonably Be Supposed to Have Arisen from Random Sampling." *Philosophical Magazine*, 1900, *50*, 157–175.

Roy, S. N., and Kastenbaum, M. A. "On the Hypothesis of 'No Interaction' in a Multi-Way Contingency Table." *Annals of Mathematical Statistics*, 1956, *27*, 749–757.

SAS Institute, Inc. *SAS User's Guide: Statistics, Version 5 Edition.* Cary, N.C.: SAS Institute, Inc., 1985.

SPSS, Inc. *SPSSX User's Guide.* (2nd ed.) Chicago, Ill.: SPSS, Inc., 1986.

Yule, G. U. "On the Association of Attributes in Statistics: With Illustration from the Material of the Childhood Society." *Philosophy Transactions of the Royal Society*, Series A, 1900, *194*, 257–319.

Dennis E. Hinkle is professor of educational research at Virginia Polytechnic Institute and State University. He has published two textbooks on applied statistics and numerous articles on statistical applications. He is currently directing the university's undergraduate student assessment program.

Gerry W. McLaughlin is associate director for institutional research and planning analysis at Virginia Polytechnic Institution and State University. His current interests include applied analytical methodology, distributed institutional research support of decision systems, and the data-information-intelligence support of organizational management. He is a member of the Association for Institutional Research (AIR), CAUSE, and Society of College and University Planners (SCUP).

James T. Austin is a National Institute of Mental Health (NIMH) postdoctoral trainee in quantitative psychology at the University of Illinois in Champaign–Urbana. His interest lies in industrial and quantitative areas, with an emphasis on the study of goals.

Regression analysis is one of the most frequently used statistical
techniques by institutional researchers. To avoid the misuse of
this family of techniques, certain guidelines should be followed.

Applying Regression Analysis to Problems in Institutional Research

Tom R. Bohannon

Institutional researchers have applied a collection of statistical techniques, called *regression analysis*, to a variety of problems. These techniques are useful in addressing problems when one or more of the following outcomes are desired: predicting, screening or selecting important variables, and studying the relationship between variables in a system. The number of professional papers and books on these techniques shows the tremendous increase of interest in the statistical techniques of regression analysis. The growth of computer capabilities and the availability of statistical software for applying these techniques contribute to this heightened interest. Since the choice of techniques may be confusing at times, this chapter provides some general guidelines to follow in performing regression analysis.

Regression analysis is a set of statistical techniques for examining and modeling relationships between variables. The analyst proposes a model to describe the relationship between the dependent variable, independent variable or variables, and parameters. Regression models are expressed in algebraic form, with the dependent variable as a function of independent variables and parameters. The parameters are unknown con-

B. D. Yancey (ed.). *Applying Statistics in Institutional Research.*
New Directions for Institutional Research, no. 58. San Francisco: Jossey-Bass, Summer 1988.

stants called *regression coefficients* that are estimated to yield the best fit of the data. The criterion we use to estimate the parameters is called the *sum-of-squares error criterion*, and the estimates are called *least squares estimates*. These estimates minimize the sum-of-squares error for the model.

This chapter presents a discussion of the principles of least squares, model building, residual analysis, influence statistics, and multicollinearity. To illustrate these concepts and techniques, examples drawn from institutional research are presented. The Statistical Analysis System (SAS; a registered trademark of SAS Institute Inc., Box 8000, Cary, N.C. 27511-8000) is utilized to analyze the data in these examples, and a discussion of some options and tests available in SAS is also presented. Obviously, these topics cannot be covered in depth in a single chapter; therefore, the interested reader is referred to the list of references for further readings. For a more detailed discussion on the use of SAS in regression analysis, the reader is referred to Freund and Littell (1986).

Much of the discussion in the following pages relates to the use, development, and evaluation of models. To begin, assume a researcher is attempting to establish a relationship between the following measures:

Y : Freshman Grade Point Average (GPA)
X_1: Scholastic Aptitude Test (SAT) Math score
X_2: SAT Verbal score
X_3: High school GPA

In this situation, Y is the dependent variable with X_1, X_2, and X_3 as independent variables. One model that could be used to describe the relationship between these variables is

$$Y = B_0 + B_1X_1 + B_2X_2 + B_3X_3 + \text{ERROR}.$$

In this expression, B_0, B_1, B_2, and B_3 are unknown and must be estimated from observed values using the least squares criterion. The error term is required since the model is not exact; that is, there is not a perfect fit between the observed values and the model.

Least Squares

The principle of least squares is applied to a set of n observed values of Y and the associated values of X_1, X_2, and X_3, to obtain estimates of the parameters B_0, B_1, B_2, and B_3. These estimates are then used to construct the following regression equation:

$$\hat{Y} = \hat{B}_0 + \hat{B}_1X_1 + \hat{B}_2X_2 + \hat{B}_3X_3.$$

In this equation $\hat{Y}$ is the predicted value of Y and is expressed as a linear combination of X_1, X_2, and X_3. The differences between the observed values and predicted values $(Y - \hat{Y})$ are called the *residuals*. The least squares procedure, which minimizes the sum of the squared residuals, finds the estimates of B_0, B_1, B_2, and B_3. Geometrically, least squares minimizes the sum of squares of the vertical distances between each observed value and the value of the regression equation.

Assumptions in Least Squares Multiple Regression

The assumptions made in least squares multiple regression are very rigid and are rarely met in practice. Those assumptions are (1) the dependent variable is measured with all the independent variables controlled or at least fixed; that is, the data come from a statistically designed experiment, (2) the form of the model has been specified correctly, (3) the mean or expected value of the errors is zero, (4) the variance of the errors is constant across observations, (5) the errors are uncorrelated, and (6) for hypothesis testing, the errors are assumed to be normally distributed.

Often the application of regression analysis to observed data does not satisfy all the preceding assumptions; in fact, rarely are all assumptions met. This does not mean that regression cannot be used; however, it does mean that one must carefully test all assumptions and cautiously draw any conclusions. In certain situations remedies (for example, transformations) can compensate for or reduce the impact of violations of some of the assumptions.

Generally, regression analysis is performed by a computer program with procedures that check these assumptions. Many computer programs perform the following tasks: estimating regression coefficients, estimating the variance of the error term, estimating the variance of the parameter estimates, testing hypotheses about the parameters, predicting values by using the estimates, evaluating the fit or lack of fit of the model, calculating residuals, calculating descriptive and diagnostic statistics.

Simple Linear Regression

A model with a single independent variable X, which defines the relationship between the dependent variable Y and X as a straight line, is called a simple *linear regression model*. This regression model is $Y = B_0 + B_1X + E$, where the intercept B_0 and the slope B_1 are the unknown parameters, and E represents the random error. For each value of X, these errors are assumed to be uncorrelated and normally distributed with a mean of zero and a constant variance.

Example 1. A researcher is attempting to establish a relationship between SAT total scores and American College Testing Program (ACT) composite scores for students entering University XYZ. The ACT score, which is the independent variable, will be used to predict the SAT score for prospective students. Twenty-five students who have both SAT and ACT scores are randomly selected. Examination of the scatter diagram, a plot of the ordered pairs (x,y), suggests a simple linear relationship between the two variables.

The regression analysis for this example was performed by **PROC REG** in the SAS system. The output from this procedure is shown in Figure 1 and numbers have been added to key the descriptions that follow.

1. This column gives the degrees of freedom for the sources of variation—model, error, and totals.

2. The sums of squares associated with the sources of variation are given and illustrate the following relationship:

Total sums of squares =
(Model sums of squares) + (Error sums of squares).

The variation in the values of SAT can be attributed to two sources: the variation due to changes in the independent variable ACT and the variation due to random error, assuming the model is correctly specified. If the model is not correct, then the variation in ACT could be attributed to some source not in the model and not just random error.

3. The associated mean squares are the sums of squares divided by their degrees of freedom. If the model is correct, the mean square for error is an unbiased estimate of the variance of the error.

Figure 1. Simple Line Regression

```
Model: MODEL1
Dep Variable: SAT
                            Analysis of Variance
                  1     2            3              4
                        Sum of       Mean
Source            DF    Squares      Square         F Value     Prob>F

Model             1  3029557.3751  3029557.3751    166.745     0.0001
Error            23   417881.66492   18168.76804
C Total          24  3447439.0400

                        5                          6
          Root MSE     134.79157    R-Square      0.8788
          Dep Mean     859.72000    Adj R-Sq      0.8735
          C.V.          15.67854    Parameter Estimates

                        7            8              9
                        Parameter    Standard       T for H0:
Variable    DF          Estimate     Error          Parameter=0   PROB>|T|
INTERCEP     1          -391.755425  100.59553427    -3.894       0.0007
ACT          1           13.782769     1.06735681    12.913       0.0001
```

4. The *F* value is the ratio of the model mean square divided by the error mean square. The value tests the hypothesis that $B_1 = 0$ and indicates the probability of obtaining this *F* value or a larger value if B_1 were equal to zero. Thus, a small probability value would indicate that the model is adequate in terms of identifying the sources of the variation in the dependent variable. In this example, the value is .0001, which indicates that we can conclude B_1 is not zero.

5. The root MSE is the square root of the mean squares error, which is an unbiased estimate of the variance of the errors—if the model has been correctly specified.

6. R-square is the ratio of the model sums of squares divided by the total sums of squares and represents the percent of total variation explained by the model. R-square is the square of the multiple correlation coefficient; in the simple linear regression case, R-square is the square of the correlation between the dependent and independent variables. With our model we are explaining 87.88 percent of the variation of SAT.

7. These are the values of the regression coefficients for these data. The regression equation is

SAT = –391.755425 + 13.782765 ACT.

SAT is the predicted value of SAT for a given value of ACT.

8. This column contains the estimated standard errors of the regression coefficients, which can be used to test hypotheses and construct confidence intervals for these parameters.

9. Shown in this column are the T statistics for testing the hypothesis that each regression coefficient is zero. The next column gives the probability of obtaining these T values if the respective regression coefficients were zero. In this example, neither hypotheses would be rejected.

After examining this output, an investigation into possible violations of assumptions is in order. The most frequent violations are the following:

- The data may contain observations, called outliers, that do not belong to the population
- The model may not have been correctly specified
- The errors may not be normally distributed
- The variances may not be the same for the entire population.

The output shown in Figure 2 aids in identifying possible outliers and influential observations. Numbered subheadings have been added to the output to key the following discussion.

1. This column gives the actual values of the dependent variable for each observation in the sample.

2. These numbers are the set of values predicted with the estimated regression equation.

Figure 2. Aids for Identifying Possible Outliers and Influential Observations

Obs	Predict SAT 1	Std Err Value 2	Predict 3	Std Err Residual 4	Residual
1	509.0	214.7	56.763	294.3	122.257
2	967.0	1014.1	29.490	-47.0870	131.526
3	921.0	986.5	28.691	-65.5215	131.703
4	1486.0	1372.4	47.993	113.6	125.958
5	455.0	614.4	32.980	-159.4	130.695
6	593.0	559.3	35.611	33.7444	130.002
7	820.0	903.8	27.174	-83.8249	132.024
8	640.0	779.8	27.660	-139.8	131.923
9	440.0	600.6	33.607	-160.6	130.535
10	421.0	586.8	34.255	-165.8	130.366
11	430.0	200.9	57.704	229.1	121.815
12	1472.0	1317.3	44.525	154.7	127.225
13	448.0	269.8	53.044	178.2	123.916
14	1167.0	1138.1	34.520	28.8681	130.296
15	436.0	504.1	38.537	-68.1246	129.165
16	1472.0	1372.4	47.993	99.6	125.958
17	1386.0	1262.2	41.208	123.8	128.338
18	1201.0	1165.7	35.892	35.3025	129.925
19	908.0	972.7	28.343	-64.7387	131.778
20	696.0	821.1	27.123	-125.1	132.034
21	581.0	724.6	28.917	-143.6	131.653
22	551.0	697.1	29.755	-146.1	131.466
23	1181.0	1151.9	35.196	29.0853	130.115
24	1081.0	1083.0	32.027	-2.0009	130.931
25	1231.0	1179.5	36.605	51.5198	129.726

Obs	Student Residual 5	-2-1-0 1 2 6	Cook's D 7
1	2.407	| |**** |	0.625
2	-0.358	| | |	0.003
3	-0.497	| | |	0.006
4	0.902	| |* |	0.059
5	-1.220	| **| |	0.047
6	0.260	| | |	0.003
7	-0.635	| *| |	0.009
8	-1.060	| **| |	0.025
9	-1.230	| **| |	0.050
10	-1.272	| **| |	0.056
11	1.881	| |*** |	0.397
12	1.216	| |** |	0.091
13	1.438	| |** |	0.189
14	0.222	| | |	0.002
15	-0.527	| *| |	0.012
16	0.790	| |* |	0.045
17	0.965	| |* |	0.048
18	0.272	| | |	0.003
19	-0.491	| | |	0.006
20	-0.948	| *| |	0.019
21	-1.091	| **| |	0.029
22	-1.111	| **| |	0.032
23	0.224	| | |	0.002
24	-0.015	| | |	0.000
25	0.397	| | |	0.006

Sum of Residuals   -2.38742E-12
Sum of Squared Residuals   417881.6649
Predicted Resid SS (Press)   536561.1042

3. As the column heading indicates, these values are the estimated standard errors of the predicted values.

4. The residuals are the differences between the actual values and the predicted values. Large values signal further examination of these observations is needed. Possible problems include the following: the data values associated with the large residuals could have been miscoded, there could have been measurement errors, or the model could be incorrect.

5. Student residual is the residual divided by the standard error. These values are approximately distributed as a t distribution. *Values greater than 2.5 should be investigated.*

6. The plot indicates the number of standard deviations the student residuals are from zero and can be useful for identifying outliers.

7. The values in this column give a measure of the influence of each observation. An observation is influential if omission of the observation from the analysis produces a large change in the estimated coefficients. Cook's D (Weisberg, 1985) is a statistic that measures this change and large values are an indication of influential observations. As noted by Bowerman, O'Connell, and Dickey (1986), "large" can be defined in terms of the twentieth and fiftieth percentiles of the F distribution with k and $n-k$ degrees of freedom, where k is the number of independent variables in the model. If the value of the statistic is less than the twentieth percentile, then the observation is not considered influential. The closer the value is to the fiftieth percentile, the more influence of the observation. If the value is greater than the fiftieth percentile, then the observation is considered influential. In our example there are no large values.

Residual Analysis

Since residuals are the deviation between the observed data and the predicted values generated by the regression model, residuals give a measure of the variability in the data not explained by the regression model and are estimates of the errors. Careful analysis of residuals helps check regression assumptions. In particular, residual plots help determine the following assumption violations: (1) Normality assumptions can be examined by looking at a normal probability plot of residuals. Most computer programs have procedures that will automatically generate these plots. If the normality assumption has not been violated, then the points would lie approximately on a straight line. The normality assumptions may also be checked by producing a histogram of the residuals for large samples. (2) A plot of the residuals against the predicted values also helps determine if the errors are random, if the variance for the errors are constant, or if the model is linear. If the errors are random, the plot of the residuals would appear as a horizontal band symmetric about zero.

Departures from these assumptions would yield plots following other patterns. A funnel-shaped pattern would indicate the variance is not constant. A complete description and interpretation of these various patterns is found in the books listed in the references, with additional examples provided in Chapter Seven of this volume.

Influence Analysis

Influence analysis studies the changes in the regression equation when an observation or observations are omitted from the analysis. To measure the changes, several statistics and techniques have been developed; Cook's D is one such statistic. However, there is no "best statistic or technique," so the analyst must select the most useful methods and become experienced and skillful with those methods. Belsley, Kuh, and Welsch (1980) discuss the statistics and techniques to measure changes in the regression equation, and the interested reader should refer to this discussion. These statistics are calculated by SAS when the INFLUENCE option is specified in the MODEL statement of PROC REG. After an influential observation has been detected, the analyst must then decide what action to take. Whether or not to remove this observation from the analysis should be based upon careful examination of the data collection and recording process. The observation should not be deleted unless there is strong evidence that the observation was the result of some unusual but explainable event such as a measurement or recording error.

Since the use of residual plots requires skill and experience to interpret, the researcher may prefer some of the statistical tests mentioned in Draper and Smith (1981). The residual plot given in Figure 3 is for the data from Example 1. This plot has a curved pattern, indicating a nonlinear relationship in the data and suggesting that a second order term should be added to the model—in this case, ACT^2. Thus, the analysis is repeated using the following model:

$$SAT = B_0 + B_1ACT + B_2ACT^2 + E$$

This model produces an improvement in the fit of the data to the model, as indicated by a larger adjusted R-square (0.9790 versus 0.8735) and a smaller mean square error (3,018.12883 versus 18,168.76804). Also, examination of the residuals from this model indicates a better fit of the data. Assuming the analyst is satisfied with the model, the next step is to examine the data for outliers and influential observations.

Multiple Linear Regression

In the previous example, the regression model involved one independent variable and was called a simple linear regression model. A

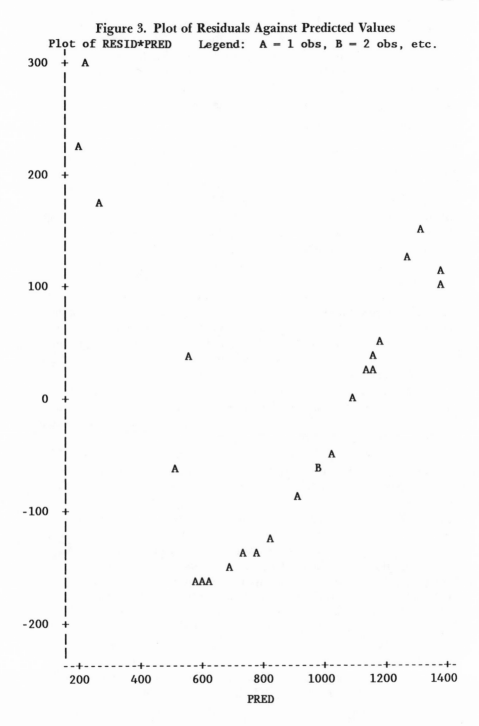

Figure 3. Plot of Residuals Against Predicted Values

model that involves more than one independent variable is called a *multiple regression model,* which is more likely to occur in institutional research than the simple linear independent model. In this context the researcher must consider selecting the "best" subset of independent variables and problems of multicollinearity—two concerns discussed in the following pages and illustrated with an example.

Variable Selection

A variable selection procedure selects the subset of independent variables whose estimated equation produces the best fit. The best fit is defined in terms of the minimum residual sum of squares or, equivalently, the maximum coefficient of determination, R^2. If the number of possible independent variables is less than twenty, then one should examine all possible subsets and select an optimum subset. Several regression packages allow this option. PROC RSQUARE in SAS is such a procedure and will be illustrated with an example. If examining all possible subsets is not feasible, then the analyst may use one sequential variable selection procedure such as forward selection, backward selection, or stepwise selection. These procedures have been criticized for various reasons, the most common being that no procedures can guarantee the "best" model will be selected. For a discussion of the advantages and disadvantages associated with these procedures, the interested reader is referred to Montgomery and Peck (1982).

To compare models generated from selected subsets of independent variables, the analyst should look at several criteria. The coefficient of determination (R^2) and the residual mean square have already been mentioned, but the analyst should not use either as the sole criterion for selecting the best model. Another criterion is the PRESS statistic, which should be considered if the primary purpose of the model is prediction of future observations. In calculating the PRESS statistic, all observations except the ith one are used to compute the regression equation and to predict Y_i. This is repeated for all n observations. Next, the difference between the observed value of the dependent variable Y_i and the predicted value of Y_i is squared and then summed. In selecting the best model, the analyst might choose the model with the smallest PRESS. Mallow's C(P) (Weisberg, 1985) statistic is also useful for selecting the best subset and will be discussed with the next example.

The choice of a final model based upon any criteria is not clear cut; however, the analyst should answer the following questions:
- Does the regression equation appear to be reasonable?
- Will the regression equation meet the user's needs?
- Do the regression coefficients seem reasonable; that is, do they have the correct sign and relative magnitude?
- Are diagnostic checks for the model satisfactory?

Multicollinearity

When selecting the independent variables to include in a model, the analyst must not create problems with multicollinearity by including too many variables. Multicollinearity is defined as a high degree of correlation among independent variables. For example, a number of the independent variables may be measuring the same phenomena and hence providing redundant information. The existence of multicollinearity generally inflates the variance of the parameter estimates and often results in coefficient estimates with incorrect signs. For more information, Myers (1986) discusses these topics.

To assess the pairwise correlations between independent variables, the analyst can examine the correlation matrix of the independent variables. However, multicollinearity may involve associations among multiple independent variables; that is, one independent variable may provide the same information as a combination of several other variables in the model. These correlations are difficult to detect. To assist in determining which variable may be involved in multicollinearities, variance inflation factors are examined. For the nth coefficient, the variance inflation factor is defined as $1/(1 - R_i^2)$, where R_i^2 is the coefficient of determination of the regression of the nth independent variable on all other independent variables. Myers (1986) indicates no rule of thumb, but generally if any variance inflation factor exceeds ten, there is reason for some concern.

Multiple Regression Example and Discussion

The following example and discussion illustrate the concepts and procedures presented in this chapter. As with the simple regression example, procedures in the SAS system will be utilized in the analysis, and portions of the output will be presented with comments.

Example 2. A researcher at University XYZ identified and collected data on several variables for freshmen entering the university. The researcher is attempting to establish a relationship between the variables and the GPAs of these freshmen after their first semester. Data were collected on these placement and personality test scores: SAT Math, SAT Verbal, Test of Standard Written English (TSWE), and high school GPA. In this example, the data were not collected from a statistically designed experiment in which the dependent variables could be controlled. As mentioned earlier, this situation frequently occurs in institutional research, and the researcher will attempt to identify all potential independent variables used to predict GPA. In another situation, the researcher will design an experiment to collect the data and thus will not be limited to the variables and data already existing in the data base. In either situation, the researcher should conduct some preliminary research on the problem and attempt to establish a list of potential dependent variables.

One of the first steps in using regression analysis is to perform exploratory data analysis. This involves the following steps: examine a listing of the data values, calculate simple univariate statistics, calculate correlations between the variables, and produce scatter plots. The SAS output shown in Figure 4 is a result of some exploratory analysis on the data in the example.

The exploratory analysis identifies miscoded data values and also gives the analyst a feel for the data. For example, in looking at the correlations, all independent variables have a fairly high correlation with GPA. However, the high correlations among the independent variables could lead to problems with multicollinearity. After the exploratory analysis and data cleanup is completed, the researcher must decide which variables to select as the dependent variables for the multiple linear regression model. Perhaps the researcher might begin by including all of the variables in the model. The output shown in Figure 5 is from **PROC REG** with all variables included in the model.

Figure 4. Step One: Exploratory Data Analysis

VARIABLE	N	MEAN	STD DEV	SUM	MINIMUM	MAXIMUM
PERTEST	682	84.6320	20.29549	57719.0	22.0000	130.0000
SATV	682	437.6100	95.69902	298450.0	200.0000	730.0000
SATM	682	493.4751	99.81234	336550.0	260.0000	740.0000
TSWE	682	45.8152	9.25592	31246.0	20.0000	60.0000
GPA	682	2.4726	0.54272	1686.3	0.9234	3.8142
TEST	682	60.8286	13.20885	41485.1	25.9258	100.9934
HISGPA	661	3.3769	0.54064	2232.1	1.2500	4.0000

PEARSON CORRELATION COEFFICIENTS
/ PROB > |R| UNDER H0:RHO=0 / NUMBER OF OBSERVATIONS

	PERTEST	SATV	SATM	TSWE	GPA	TEST	HISGPA
PERTEST	1.00000	0.80091	0.76270	0.70327	0.78690	0.88866	0.48145
	0.0000	0.0001	0.0001	0.0001	0.0001	0.0001	0.0001
	682	682	682	682	682	682	661
SATV	0.80091	1.00000	0.59709	0.71694	0.61831	0.97043	0.37523
	·0.0001	0.0000	0.0001	0.0001	0.0001	0.0001	0.0001
	682	682	682	682	682	682	661
SATM	0.76270	0.59709	1.00000	0.56522	0.92593	0.66397	0.44625
	0.0001	0.0001	0.0000	0.0001	0.0001	0.0001	0.0001
	682	682	682	682	682	682	661
TSWE	0.70327	0.71694	0.56522	1.00000	0.56076	0.73226	0.36921
	0.0001	0.0001	0.0001	0.0000	0.0001	0.0001	0.0001
	682	682	682	682	682	682	661
GPA	0.78690	0.61831	0.92593	0.56076	1.00000	0.68507	0.43202
	0.0001	0.0001	0.0001	0.0001	0.0000	0.0001	0.0001
	682	682	682	682	682	682	661
TEST	0.88866	0.97043	0.66397	0.73226	0.68507	1.00000	0.40778
	0.0001	0.0001	0.0001	0.0001	0.0001	0.0000	0.0001
	682	682	682	682	682	682	661
HISGPA	0.48145	0.37523	0.44625	0.36921	0.43202	0.40778	1.00000
	0.0001	0.0001	0.0001	0.0001	0.0001	0.0001	0.0000
	661	661	661	661	661	661	661

1. The degrees of freedom for the model is equal to the number of variables in the model. The number of observations included in the analysis is 661, and the degrees of freedom for the total is one less or 660.

2. The F value for testing the model is very large and tests the hypothesis that $B_1 = B_2 = B_3 = B_4 = B_5 = B_6 = 0$ against the hypothesis that at least one of the B_i is not zero. The hypothesis that all the B_i are zero is rejected for this model.

3. For this analysis R-square and adjusted R-square are very high.

4. The regression equation is

GPA = -.001081469 - .004220677 (TEST) + .00646711 (PERTEST) + .000505587 (SATV) + .004254707 (SATM) - .002120993 (TSWE) - .01213915 (HISGPA).

5. The T values are used to test between two models. For example, the T value for TEST is used to test the hypothesis that the coefficient of TEST in the model is zero. Thus the two models in question are the

Figure 5. Multiple Regression Using PROC REG

DEP VARIABLE: GPA   ANALYSIS OF VARIANCE

SOURCE	DF	SUM OF SQUARES	MEAN SQUARE	F VALUE	PROB>F
MODEL	6	168.39424	28.06570734	767.584	0.0001
ERROR	654	23.91265980	0.03656370		
C TOTAL	660	192.30690			

ROOT MSE	0.1912164	R-SQUARE	0.8757	
DEP MEAN	2.474996	ADJ R-SQ	0.8745	
C.V.	7.725925			

PARAMETER ESTIMATES

VARIABLE	DF	PARAMETER ESTIMATE	STANDARD ERROR	T FOR H0: PARAMETER=0	PROB > |T|
INTERCEP	1	-0.001081469	0.05512875	-0.020	0.9844
TEST	1	-0.004220677	0.003715357	-1.136	0.2564
PERTEST	1	0.006467110	0.001112102	5.815	0.0001
SATV	1	0.000504487	0.000395162	1.277	0.2022
SATM	1	0.004254707	0.000118034	36.046	0.0001
TSWE	1	-0.002120993	0.001217384	-1.742	0.0819
HISGPA	1	-0.01213915	0.01595075	-0.761	0.4469

VARIABLE	DF	TOLERANCE	VARIANCE INFLATION
INTERCEP	1	.	0
TEST	1	0.02287275	43.72014116
PERTEST	1	0.10823526	9.23913333
SATV	1	0.03852656	25.95612175
SATM	1	0.40428779	2.47348553
TSWE	1	0.43706079	2.28801125
HISGPA	1	0.74494004	1.34238992

model with TEST and the model without TEST. In this example, the hypothesis that the coefficient is equal to zero is not rejected.

6. Two of the variance inflation factors are very high. This is an indication that collinearity exists.

Additional diagnostic procedures are performed by PROC REG when the COLLINOINT option is invoked. For a more detailed discussion of this analysis the reader is referred to Belsley, Kuh, and Welsch (1980). In general terms, a collinearity problem exists when a component associated with a high condition index contributes strongly to the variance of two or more variables. Note that the output shown in Figure 6, produced with all the variables in the model, indicates the analyst should consider selecting a subset of the variables.

There are several approaches to selecting a subset of variables to be used in the model. SAS has two procedures, STEPWISE and RSQUARE, that allow the analyst to choose from several different variable selection techniques. For this example, the FORWARD option of the STEPWISE procedure selects the variables: SATM, PERTEST, TSWE, and HISGPA; the BACKWARD option selects the variables: SATM, PERTEST, and TSWE. For data with collinearity, it is not unusual for variable selection techniques to yield two different subsets.

The output in Figure 7 is from RSQUARE, which finds the optimum subset for each subset size. The output provides information on R-square and C(P) for each subset of variables. C(P) gives a measure of the error variance and shows the bias the model introduces from omitting important variables. It is recommended that C(P) be plotted against $P + 1$, where P is the number of independent variables in the model. As noted

Figure 6. Diagnostic Information Using COLLINOINT Option

VARI NUMBER	EIGENVALUE	CONDITION NUMBER	VAR PROP TEST	VAR PROP PERTEST	VAR PROP SATV	VAR PROP SATM
		COLLINEARITY DIAGNOSTICS				
1	4.245327	1.000000	0.0011	0.0053	0.0018	0.0145
2	0.773697	2.342449	0.0015	0.0001	0.0038	0.0136
3	0.460143	3.037449	0.0010	0.0080	0.0061	0.5830
4	0.356950	3.448674	0.0072	0.0055	0.0149	0.0288
5	0.149965	5.320603	0.0003	0.4892	0.0472	0.3583
6	0.013918	17.464802	0.9888	0.4920	0.9263	0.0019

NUMBER	VAR PROP TSWE	VAR PROP HISGPA
1	0.0164	0.0133
2	0.0187	0.7818
3	0.1000	0.1699
4	0.8600	0.0080
5	0.0004	0.0166
6	0.0046	0.0105

Figure 7. Multiple Regression Using PROC RSQUARE

```
N=661          REGRESSION MODELS FOR DEPENDENT VARIABLE: GPA
NUMBER IN      R-SQUARE          C(P)    VARIABLES IN MODEL
MODEL
   1         0.18664373       3620.850   HISGPA
   1         0.31334368       2954.471   TSWE
   1         0.38447782       2580.341   SATV
   1         0.47487254       2104.910   TEST
   1         0.62414392       1319.816   PERTEST
   1         0.85889033         85.166771 SATM
------------------------------------------------
   2         0.37214035       2647.230   TSWE HISGPA
   2         0.41212935       2436.908   SATV TSWE
   2         0.43073425       2339.055   SATV HISGPA
   2         0.48126399       2073.294   TSWE TEST
   2         0.50222851       1963.031   HISGPA TEST
   2         0.51563166       1892.537   SATV TEST
   2         0.62418617       1321.594   PERTEST TSWE
   2         0.62451052       1319.888   PERTEST SATV
   2         0.62491008       1317.787   PERTEST TEST
   2         0.62761849       1303.542   PERTEST HISGPA
   2         0.85931560         84.930076 SATM HISGPA
   2         0.86087447         76.731186 SATM TSWE
   2         0.86583696         50.630980 SATV SATM
   2         0.86814283         38.503253 SATM TEST
   2         0.87473206          3.847165 PERTEST SATM
------------------------------------------------------
   3         0.44881332       2245.968   SATV TSWE HISGPA
   3         0.50602957       1945.039   TSWE HISGPA TEST
   3         0.52275209       1857.087   SATV TSWE TEST
   3         0.53731078       1780.516   SATV HISGPA TEST
   3         0.62471614       1320.807   PERTEST SATV TSWE
   3         0.62518946       1318.317   PERTEST TSWE TEST
   3         0.62535384       1317.453   PERTEST SATV TEST
   3         0.62763133       1305.474   PERTEST TSWE HISGPA
   3         0.62794498       1303.825   PERTEST SATV HISGPA
   3         0.62823315       1302.309   PERTEST HISGPA TEST
   3         0.86106268         77.741292 SATM TSWE HISGPA
   3         0.86585112         52.556489 SATV SATM TSWE
   3         0.86590223         52.287689 SATV SATM HISGPA
   3         0.86816550         40.383979 SATM HISGPA TEST
   3         0.86833583         39.488139 SATM TSWE TEST
   3         0.86905708         35.694737 SATV SATM TEST
   3         0.87473210          5.846948 PERTEST SATV SATM
   3         0.87475672          5.717475 PERTEST SATM TEST
   3         0.87483763          5.291911 PERTEST SATM HISGPA
   3         0.87525133          3.116057 PERTEST SATM TSWE
----------------------------------------------------------
   4         0.54191064       1758.323   SATV TSWE HISGPA TEST
   4         0.62554662       1318.439   PERTEST SATV TSWE TEST
   4         0.62806233       1305.207   PERTEST SATV TSWE HISGPA
   4         0.62839439       1303.461   PERTEST TSWE HISGPA TEST
   4         0.62849489       1302.932   PERTEST SATV HISGPA TEST
   4         0.86592248         54.181147 SATV SATM TSWE HISGPA
   4         0.86837024         41.307174 SATM TSWE HISGPA TEST
   4         0.86907334         37.609200 SATV SATM HISGPA TEST
   4         0.86919901         36.948259 SATV SATM TSWE TEST
```

58

Figure 7. *(continued)*

NUMBER IN	R-SQUARE	C(P)	VARIABLES IN MODEL
4	0.87483774	7.291307	PERTEST SATV SATM HISGPA
4	0.87486700	7.137418	PERTEST SATM HISGPA TEST
4	0.87493991	6.753973	PERTEST SATV SATM TEST
4	0.87525977	5.071687	PERTEST SATM TSWE TEST
4	0.87532608	4.722890	PERTEST SATV SATM TSWE
4	0.87533832	4.658531	PERTEST SATM TSWE HISGPA
---	---	---	---
5	0.62860725	1304.341	PERTEST SATV TSWE HISGPA TEST
5	0.86922402	38.816704	SATV SATM TSWE HISGPA TEST
5	0.87507652	8.035451	PERTEST SATV SATM HISGPA TEST
5	0.87534377	6.629856	PERTEST SATM TSWE HISGPA TEST
5	0.87540829	6.290515	PERTEST SATV SATM TSWE HISGPA
5	0.87554354	5.579181	PERTEST SATV SATM TSWE TEST
---	---	---	---
6	0.87565366	7.000000	PERTEST SATV SATM TSWE HISGPA TEST

DEP VARIABLE: GPA

ANALYSIS OF VARIANCE

SOURCE	DF	SUM OF SQUARES	MEAN SQUARE	F VALUE	PROB>F
MODEL	3	175.18530	58.39509955	1558.612	0.0001
ERROR	678	25.40201418	0.03746610		
C TOTAL	681	200.58731			

ROOT MSE	0.1935616	R-SQUARE	0.8734	
DEP MEAN	2.472638	ADJ R-SQ	0.8728	
C.V.	7.828141			

PARAMETER ESTIMATES

VARIABLE	DF	PARAMETER ESTIMATE	STANDARD ERROR	T FOR H0: PARAMETER=0	PROB > |T|
INTERCEP	1	-0.02276756	0.04258375	-0.535	0.5931
SATM	1	0.004245842	0.000115128	36.879	0.0001
TSWE	1	-0.001759365	0.001129424	-1.558	0.1198
PERTEST	1	0.005681000	0.000656997	8.647	0.0001

VARIABLE	DF	VARIANCE INFLATION	VARIABLE LABEL
INTERCEP	1	0	INTERCEPT
SATM	1	2.40016993	
TSWE	1	1.98638111	
PERTEST	1	3.23172937	SUM OF STD SCORES

COLLINEARITY DIAGNOSTICS

NUMBER	EIGENVALUE	CONDITION NUMBER	VAR PROP SATM	VAR PROP TSWE	VAR PROP PERTEST
1	2.357382	1.000000	0.0577	0.0652	0.0484
2	0.439264	2.316605	0.3776	0.6770	0.0079
3	0.203353	3.404782	0.5647	0.2579	0.9437

by Freund and Littell (1986), the most useful subset sizes are between the minimum values of C(P) and the point where C(P) becomes greater than $P + 1$. Consequently, the selected subset size should be either three or four in our example. Since there is little difference between the R-squares and the PRESS statistics for the optimum subsets, the simpler model with only three variables—SATM, PERTEST, and TSWE—is chosen for further analysis.

In the PROC REG output for the model with these variables, examination of the variance inflation factors and condition numbers give no indication of collinearity. Having selected the model, the analyst should next examine the data for influential observations.

Summary

As illustrated by the examples, some general guidelines should be followed for an effective approach to regression analysis. First, the analyst must understand the background of the problem and know how the data were collected. Second, the analyst should perform exploratory analysis on the data and then begin the process of selecting the variables to enter into the model, which involves checking the collinearity effects of the proposed model. Third, the analyst should look at residual plots and regression diagnostics to check the adequacy of the model. Fourth, the analyst should also check for influential observations and, if any are found, make some decision regarding those observations. Finally, the model that results from this process should be monitored, updated, and modified when necessary.

References

Belsley, D. A., Kuh, E., and Welsch, R. E. *Regression Diagnostics: Identifying Influential Data and Sources of Collinearity.* New York: Wiley, 1980.

Bowerman, B. L., O'Connell, R., and Dickey, D. A. *Linear Statistical Models.* Boston: Duxbury Press, 1986.

Draper, N. R., and Smith, H. *Applied Regression Analysis.* New York: Wiley, 1981.

Freund, R. J., and Littell, R. C. *SAS System for Regression.* Cary, N.C.: SAS Institute, Inc., 1986.

Montgomery, D. L., and Peck, E. A. *Introduction to Linear Regression Analysis.* New York: Wiley, 1982.

Myers, R. H. *Classical and Modern Regression with Applications.* Boston: PWS and Kent Publishing, 1986.

SAS Institute, Inc. *SAS User's Guide: Statistics, Version 5 Edition.* Cary, N.C.: SAS Institute, Inc., 1985.

Weisberg, S. *Applied Linear Regression.* New York: Wiley, 1985.

Tom R. Bohannon is director of institutional research and testing at Baylor University and also teaches training courses for SAS Institute, Inc. His interests include development and utilization of university data bases to support decision making and the use of statistical methods and modeling in institutional research.

Causal modeling methods such as path analysis and linear structural relations (LISREL) can be useful to institutional researchers.

Causal Modeling for Institutional Researchers

Arlett E. Moline

Educators and other social science researchers are just beginning to discover the potential usefulness of *causal modeling* methods. Causal modeling is the application of methods that test hypothesized theoretical relationships among variables. *Structural equation modeling* and *analysis of covariance structures* are other terms frequently used for this approach. Since institutional researchers frequently conduct field studies involving the relationships of many variables to a dependent variable (as well as to one another), a multivariate methodology such as causal modeling can be useful. Causal modeling relates theory and data and helps researchers pursue the complex phenomena of the educational experience.

Causal modeling methodologies have been used for some time in the fields of biology, economics, and sociology. Causal modeling was used as early as 1918 by geneticist Sewall Wright (1921), who then formally presented his ideas in an article three years later. In spite of its early origin, causal modeling was not popularized in the social sciences until the publication of a significant paper by Duncan (1966). Causal modeling has been further presented in the writings of Land (1969), Blalock (1971, 1972), and Kenny (1979). Only more recently has causal modeling been considered in the education context (Anderson, 1978; Pascarella and Terenzini, 1983; and Wolfle, 1977, 1980, 1985).

B. D. Yancey (ed.). *Applying Statistics in Institutional Research.*
New Directions for Institutional Research, no. 58. San Francisco: Jossey-Bass, Summer 1988.

Causal modeling methods need to be part of the research strategies available to the institutional researcher. Researchers must know about these techniques in order to recognize when they are appropriate and useful and to understand and evaluate the reported research studies that employ causal analysis.

Causation

Although researchers have long been skeptical about the concept of causation, they frequently reflect causation in both their terminology and methodology. Researchers use causal terminology whenever they say that one variable "affects" or "influences" another variable. Likewise, when a research methodology "partials out variance" or determines "true score variance," the concept of causation is implied.

Three commonly accepted conditions must hold to show causation: (1) time precedence, (2) relationship, and (3) nonspuriousness (Kenny, 1979). Time precedence means that X must precede Y in time. Relationship means a functional relationship must exist between X and Y; that is, when the variables are covariant and one variable changes in value, the other also changes in a systematic or consistent way. Nonspuriousness describes a relationship between X and Y that does not vanish when the effect of another variable or set of variables is controlled.

Experimental researchers have developed ways to manipulate independent variables in experimental studies, effecting or causing change in the dependent variables. These researchers use this type of control of variables, as well as the control by random assignment, to study causation.

The nonexperimental (or field) researcher studies events in their natural surroundings and does not usually have available the experimental researcher's methods. Nonexperimental events are frequently complex phenomena that the researcher cannot manipulate or randomize to exert control. Although correlation is not proof of causation, the nonexperimental researcher may use the correlations, or covariation, among variables to suggest the presence of causal linkages, proceeding as if the theorized causal relations exist.

Causal Modeling

Causal modeling is a method of hypothesis testing that looks at theorized causal relationships among variables. Causal modeling techniques, heuristic devices that help the researcher describe and understand the system of linkages between and among variables, shift the emphasis from single variables of interest to patterns of variables and their effect on a particular dependent variable. Causal modeling allows the decomposition of effects into direct and indirect effects, a process which provides a rich yield of parameters in the interpretation of the underlying structure of the model. Causal modeling is also used "to provide quantitative estimates of the impacts of causes on their effects, and to interpret these coefficients in the context of the theory being expressed in the model" (Wolfle, 1985, p. 385).

A major benefit of causal modeling is to force a clarity of thinking that may not be otherwise present. To use the methodology, a specific a priori causal model must be defined. A good researcher probably has some implicit or subconscious theory in mind, and the a priori construction of a theory is merely a specification of the key variables and their presumed relationships. As pointed out by Asher (1983), "thinking causally about a problem and constructing a . . . diagram that reflects causal processes may often facilitate the clearer statement of hypotheses and the generation of additional insights into the topic at hand" (p. 8).

Causal modeling begins with a theory specifying the relationships among the variables. It is theory, not data, that builds the model. "An explanatory scheme is not arrived at on the basis of the data, but rather on the basis of knowledge, theoretical formulations and assumptions, and logical analysis" (Pedhazur, 1982, p. 579).

In designing a causal modeling study, the order of specific steps is important.

1. Identify the relevant variables in the theory.
2. Formulate a theory of the relationships between the variables.
3. Construct a model to display the patterns of the causal relationships among the variables.
4. Collect data on the variables.
5. Analyze the fit of the model to the data.

The model determines the type of data to be collected and the technique by which the data are analyzed. After the model is specified, the data are analyzed to compare the model to the data to see if the fit is close, thereby indicating if the model is consistent with the data and should be retained. If the fit is not close then the model must be revised or a new model proposed.

If the theory is consistent with the data, then the theory withstood the test: it is not disconfirmed. If the model is supported, this is a plausible model, but one of several that may fit the data since alternative models may also be consistent with the data. Causal modeling merely checks whether the correlational data are consistent with the proposed causal model; it does not prove the model is "true."

Duncan (1975) divides the work of causal modeling into the easy part (statistical analysis of the model) and the hard part (construction of the theoretical model). The causal modeling techniques are merely analytic tools in the assessment and interpretation of the model, so when the theoretical model is inaccurate, a complex statistical analysis is worthless.

Techniques of Causal Modeling

When fitting the model to the data, the researcher must choose among different techniques, several of which estimate the parameters of the model (that is, the strengths of the relations among the variables in the model). Two of the most frequently applied techniques will be discussed: path analysis using ordinary least squares multiple regression and linear structural relations (LISREL) using maximum likelihood.

The choice of technique to assess the fit of the model depends on the characteristics of the a priori model that depicts the relationships among the variables. The researcher's explanatory scheme determines the type of analysis, and not vice versa.

The model depicting the relationships among the variables is characterized as either *recursive* or *nonrecursive*. In a recursive model, the causal flow is unidirectional; there are no feedback loops. An example of a recursive relationship is between sex and grade point average (GPA); sex may affect GPA, but GPA does not affect sex. Path analysis may be an appropriate technique when the model is recursive. If the model is nonrecursive, there is presumed reciprocal causation between variables (for example, as GPA goes up, satisfaction goes up; as satisfaction goes up, GPA goes up), and different procedures estimate the parameters of the model. Nonrecursive models cannot be analyzed by least squares regression because there may be residuals correlated with the variables; this analysis would violate the assumptions of least squares regression and result in biased and inconsistent estimates. LISREL is the most widely used method for analyzing nonrecursive models.

However, other characteristics of the model such as use of single or multiple indicators of the variables must also be considered before making a final choice of method.

Path Analysis

Path analysis, a heuristic method of comparing hypothesized patterns of direct and indirect relationships among variables with observed data, uses correlational data to examine the plausibility of hypotheses about causal relationships among variables in a theory. The advantages of path analysis over the usual regression analysis is it allows the decomposition of effects and provides a way of interpreting and studying complex phenomena with multiple variables. Wright (1934) states that "the method of path coefficients is not intended to accomplish the impossible task of deducing causal relations from the values of the correlation coefficients. It is intended to combine the quantitative information given by the correlations with such qualitative information as may be at hand on causal relations to give a quantitative interpretation" (p. 193).

Path analysis, using standardized regression coefficients to describe a theoretical model, sometimes requires a series of regressions. At each stage, a dependent variable is regressed on the independent variables that are logically and/or temporally prior.

Each multiple regression equation provides a set of standardized regression coefficients or beta weights (see Chapter Four), which are the net effect of an independent variable on a dependent variable after considering all other independent variables in the model. The advantage is that standardized regression coefficients are scale free, which means the ability to compare the relative importance of the variables in the model for a single population.

The standardized beta weights assess the relative importance of the independent variables in explaining variance in the dependent variable. The beta is the amount of change in the dependent variable that is associated with one standard deviation unit change in the independent variable when all other variables are held constant. The beta size is the relative magnitude of the influence, and the beta sign indicates whether the relationship between the two variables is positive or negative. The level of statistical significance of each beta is also obtained.

Standardized betas cannot be used when comparisons are made across populations because the betas are relative only to the specific standardized population. For comparisons across models, populations, or the same population over time, unstandardized betas (which are in metric and not Z score form) must be used. When the objective is to predict the actual value of an interval-level criterion variable, standardized betas are used. An example of this is predicting the need for more classrooms.

Path analysis allows the decomposition of total effects into direct and indirect effects. Direct effects are standardized regression coefficients or beta weights for each variable: the effect of an independent variable on a dependent variable. Indirect effects represent the influences of each causal variable on the dependent variable that are mediated through other variables in the model. Indirect effects are estimated by the sum of the products of direct causal effects through intervening variables. The total effect of a variable is the sum of the direct and indirect effects.

Path analysis also provides an R^2 for the model, an indication of the theoretical model's total explanatory power. The R^2 indicates the percentage of the variance in the dependent variable, which is explained by all independent variables in the model working together.

Assumptions. The assumptions that underlie the use of path analysis (see Chapter Four) include the usual assumptions of multiple regression in addition to specific assumptions on testing causal models.

1. Relations among variables in the model are linear, additive, and causal. Interactive relations within the model are excluded. Variables are not highly correlated with each other.

2. Variables are measured on at least an interval scale.

3. A one-way causal flow in the system means there is no reciprocal causation between variables: no feedback loops. The model is recursive.

4. No residual is correlated with the variables that precede it in the model. The implication is that "all relevant variables are included in the model that is being tested. . . . variables not included and subsumed under residuals are assumed to be not correlated with the relevant variables" (Pedhazur, 1982, p. 582). Violation of this assumption is called a specification error. When a wrong or inappropriate model is specified for analysis, the model is misspecified.

5. Variables are measured without error. A high degree of measurement reliability and validity should exist. Note that each indicator is actually treated as a perfectly reliable and valid measure of the variable.

These assumptions are discussed further in methodology textbooks (Kerlinger, 1986; Loether and McTavish, 1980; Pedhazur, 1982).

Departures from Assumptions. The reliability of the interpretation of the path analysis and the inferences made from it depend on the satisfaction of the assumptions. Certain assumptions are seldom satisfied exactly in social science research. In the real world, researchers frequently work with less than ideal conditions. Experience shows that least squares multiple regression is robust because slight departures from some assumptions may not substantially effect the results; however, certain departures or combinations of departure can produce unknown effects.

To the extent that assumptions are violated, the results may be unreliable. It is therefore important to consider each assumption and discover to what extent it has been violated before beginning the data analysis. Early modifications in the collection and treatment of data can sometimes correct situations that normally would weaken the assumptions. Variables can be mathematically transformed to stabilize the variance or to change the shape of a distribution, although sometimes constructing a whole new model is necessary.

Researchers frequently violate certain assumptions such as the use of interval-level data, whereas the violation of others such as the recursiveness of the model cannot be tolerated. Some small-to-moderate departures may not be of great concern, yet the researcher must know of the violation.

Some steps can be taken to uncover evidence of departures from assumptions:

1. The model must be carefully examined for specification error, errors committed in the specification of the model to be tested. Both the omission of relevant variables and the inclusion of irrelevant ones create problems. If the omitted relevant variables are correlated with any independent variable and a dependent variable in the model, then the estima-

tion of the coefficients in that part of the model is biased. When irrelevant variables are included (that is, they are not correlated with the dependent variable), they are treated as errors, resulting in a larger standard errors for the betas. Specification error is probably the most difficult error to detect. The theory's importance is obvious: Relevant variables are identified through theory. To eliminate misspecification, reformulating the original theory may be necessary.

2. A recursive model with a one-way causal flow between variables is also important. If the model is not recursive, then path analysis is not an appropriate method. The ordering or placement of the variables in the model may be substantiated by theoretical models, past experience, past empirical research, or temporal order. For example, temporal order is violated in a model that places the student's gender in the model after the student enrolls in college.

3. The model must be checked for interactions to see if the variables are really additive. Checking for every possible interaction in the model is usually not practical, but if there is strong indication of an interaction, then test it. For example, in student attrition studies, some researchers have suggested an interaction between the student's sex and the persistence pattern in higher education (that is, persistence patterns may vary by sex). A significance test of the F ratio for an increment in the multiple R^2 can be done between a model with direct effects and another model with both all the direct effects and all the interaction effects of sex. If interaction is found, then score the interaction as a separate variable or construct separate models of attrition for males and females.

4. Since path analysis requires independent variables not highly intercorrelated, there should be low interdependence of explanatory variables. The intercorrelations among the variables must be examined for high levels of multicollinearity between the independent variables, which cause unstable structural parameter estimates and inflated standard errors. Although still debatable, some analysts have set a correlation coefficient of .7 or .8 as the level at which to become concerned about multicollinearity (Asher, 1983, p. 52). If there is high multicollinearity, creating a scale to incorporate the correlated variables or making a change in the model to remove the problem may be necessary.

5. The construction of scatterplots checks the linearity assumption. If a relationship between variables is nonlinear, a simple transformation (such as a logarithmic transformation) might uncover a linear relationship (Norušis, 1985, pp. 32–33).

6. The plotting and study of residual errors identifies possible deviations of assumptions. The distribution of residuals provides clues to linearity, normality, and homoscedasticity (that is, variance of error terms is constant across all levels).

7. One of the most frequently violated assumptions is that variables are measured on an interval scale, using categorical or nominal-level variables. Nominal-level variables are handled in some cases by using dummy coding. When independent variables are either qualitative or categorical, they cannot be measured on a numerical interval scale but need to be coded into numbers before being entered into the regression equations. When these types of variables are recoded, they are called *dummy variables*. The construction of a two-category dummy variable usually involves the absence or presence of a characteristic. For example, a dummy variable, like sex, may be created where 1 represents male and 0 represents female. The number of dummy variables is one less than the number of categories describing the variable. These dummy variables are then treated as interval variables and entered into the regression equations (Loether and McTavish, 1980, pp. 363-365).

8. Any data more than three standard deviations from the mean in either direction should be checked for possible error. If indications of miscoding or inaccurate information exist, consider eliminating those subjects from the data.

Useful discussions of the identification and results of certain types of departure from the assumptions may be found in Pedhazur (1982, pp. 225-247) and Norušis (1985, pp. 24-55). Even though departures are frequently made, these assumptions need to be taken seriously, as the consequences of departure are open to debate and largely unknown. At the minimum, careful consideration of possible violations of assumptions allows the researcher to consider the extent of the departure.

Advantages and Disadvantages. An advantage of path analysis is its use of the familiar technique of ordinary least squares regression, which is especially attractive to researchers who already know the least squares procedures. However, the only appropriate use of path analysis is when the question to be answered is framed within the context of a recursive model.

The obvious disadvantage of path analysis is that the validity of the method requires a set of very restrictive assumptions. Many researchers claim that the assumptions are seldom met in nonexperimental research and that reality is nonrecursive in many instances. Another disadvantage is that variables are not measured without error, and systematic errors affect the validity of measures. Finally, in some research (for example, longitudinal studies), to assume that the residuals are uncorrelated is particularly unreasonable.

Example. Use of causal modeling in an educational setting is found in the studies of student persistence in higher education, when researchers assess the relative importance of numerous background and college experience variables on persistence. A study of financial aid and student persistence (Moline, 1987) will be used to illustrate path analysis. The model in this study drew heavily on Tinto's (1975) model of student attrition, but it was adapted to place more emphasis on academic variables for the study of persistence in a commuter institution. Path analysis examined the relationships among the variables, and the paths of the theoretical model that were significant in this study are presented in Figure 1.

Path analysis was appropriate because the model was recursive, and there was a single measured indicator of each variable. The analysis required three sets of regression equations. Each set included all the variables that preceded it in the model: First, each of the financial aid variables were separately regressed on the background variables; second, college GPA was regressed on the background and financial aid variables; third, credits completed (the persistence criterion) was regressed on the background, financial aid, and GPA variables.

Significant variables that showed the largest total effects on persistence were college GPA and high school rank. None of the financial aid variables had a significant direct effect on persistence in this study of financial aid recipients. The decomposition of effects showed that the Preliminary Scholastic Aptitude Test (PSAT) had no direct effect on persistence, but it did have an important indirect effect. The PSAT had a significant effect on GPA, which in turn influenced persistence. This study demonstrates the real advantage of path analysis: it allows interpretation of indirect and total effects of a model. If the method of data analysis had identified only direct effects, the PSAT would have appeared to have had no effect. Path analysis was useful in understanding the relationships between the variables in this study. Further interpretation and discussion of the path model and the study are available in Moline (1987).

LISREL

Jöreskog (1973) first introduced linear structural relations (LISREL) in its general form. Long (1983, p. 7) points out that "the importance of LISREL is evidenced by the fact that the term LISREL has come to stand for not only software but also a statistical model and an approach to data analysis." LISREL is a computer program (Jöreskog and Sörbom, 1983) that uses a maximum likelihood analysis of structural equations to look at the causal model. Maximum likelihood relies on an iterative procedure to estimate the parameters most likely to have generated the observed data.

The virtue of LISREL is its suitability to analyze the complex phenomena frequently studied by institutional researchers. LISREL does not require the numerous restrictive assumptions necessary for path analysis; therefore, it fits more realistically within the social science, non-experimental, and field environments. LISREL is extremely useful in longitudinal research, in which the same variable is measured over time. Very versatile LISREL can be used for analysis of causal models with

Figure 1. Path Model of Significant Paths for a Causal Model of
Student Persistence

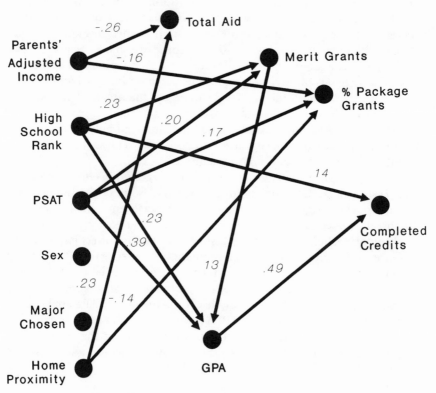

Source: Moline, 1987, p. 141.

multiple indicators of latent variables, reciprocal causation, measurement errors, correlated errors, and correlated residuals.

LISREL consists of two major parts: the structural model and the measurement or factor model. The structural model refers to the relations among the latent variables (also called unobserved variables, constructs, or true variables) in the model. LISREL allows the construction of models that include latent, unmeasured constructs as variables. Institutional researchers frequently use latent concepts such as intelligence, scholastic ability, and socioeconomic status. The measurement or factor model specifies the relations between the latent and manifest variables. Multiple manifest variables may be used as indicators of an underlying latent variable (for example, PSAT, GPA, and teacher ratings might all be considered manifest indicators of the latent variable of scholastic ability).

The LISREL model consists of the "simultaneous specification of a factor model and a structural equation model, and as such represents a fruitful unification of psychometrics and econometrics" (Long, 1983, p. 12). The factor model and the structural model provide the information for LISREL to generate estimates of all unknown parameters in the model. LISREL could be considered a combination of confirmatory factor analysis and path analysis.

In creating LISREL, Jöreskog and Sörbom (1978) combine the concepts of structural equation modeling and factor analysis and state that LISREL in its most general form assumes that "there is a causal structure among a set of latent variables or hypothetical constructs, some of which are designated as dependent variables and others as independent variables. These latent variables are not directly observed, but there is a set of observed variables that are related to the latent variables. Thus the latent variables appear as underlying causes of the observed variables" (p. 3).

LISREL uses a covariance matrix of the observed variables to estimate the elements of eight matrices by the method of maximum likelihood. These matrices provide the information necessary to decompose the total effects into direct, indirect, and noncausal effects. The matrices also provide an indication of the proportion of variance in the dependent variable left unexplained by the variables in the model and a chi square that assesses the fit of the model to the data.

Primary Assumption. The primary assumption of LISREL is that of multivariate normality. To say that the data set is multivariate normal is a very restrictive, but necessary, assumption for the chi square and the standard errors to work properly in the maximum likelihood estimates. Many institutional research variables have unknown distributions, and many deviate from normality. Wolfle (1985) cautions that "while the maximum likelihood fitting function may be used if the observed variables do not deviate too much from normality, the standard errors must be interpreted with a great deal of caution. Furthermore, deviations from normality have a substantial influence on the magnitude of the likelihood ratio chi square statistic often used to assess the fit of the model" (p. 403). However, there are methods, other than the computer program LISREL that analyzes latent variable models, that do not require the multivariate normality assumption (Bentler and Weeks, 1980).

Identification. The issue of identification, which refers to the number of fixed or known parameters—either correlations or variances, must be considered in any discussion of causal modeling. Most common among these parameters are correlations between measured variables relative to the number of parameters in the model. Identification reveals whether an estimation of the parameters of the model is possible. If more unknown parameters than known parameters exist in an equation, then the equation cannot be solved; this situation is called underidentification.

When using LISREL, researchers want the model to be just identified or, preferably, overidentified. A model is overidentified when there is more than one way to estimate a causal parameter in the system. Recursive models are always just identified, and identification is not a problem.

LISREL allows both fixed and free parameters. Fixed parameters are held at a certain value a priori, whereas free parameters are unknown and allowed to vary and be estimated by the program. An identification problem can be solved by changing the model and either fixing or freeing the values of certain parameters. Identification must be determined before beginning an analysis. For further discussion, readers are directed to Kenny, 1979, pp. 34-41.

Advantages and Disadvantages. Several advantages to using LISREL are

- Multiple indicators of the latent variables can be used to reduce the error in measurement
- Reciprocal causation is allowed in the model
- The maximum likelihood solution is at least as efficient as the least squares regression solution
- A chi square is provided so that the goodness of fit of the model to the data can be assessed
- Indexes suggest changes in the specification of the model that would improve the fit. (A note of caution: the use of these indexes begins to look like exploratory analysis and not the confirmatory work for which LISREL was intended.)

An important strength of this technique is that LISREL allows multiple indicators of each latent variable, which may reduce the measurement error. However, LISREL can also be used with single indicators of the variables. If the model has single indicators of each variable and is a recursive model, then similar results will be obtained from path analysis and LISREL. Path analysis could be considered a specific type of LISREL analysis.

In addition to the potential limitations in the application of any causal modeling method, several other potential difficulties occur that pertain specifically to LISREL. The biggest disadvantage of LISREL is the very complex language and terminology. Researchers have difficulty when trying to represent their models in the various equations and in accurately setting up the computer program. Frequent problems occur in running the program or, if it does not run, in discovering the reason for the failure. LISREL can also be difficult to interpret, especially as the model gets more complex, so a strong math background is helpful to understand LISREL.

Example. To illustrate a situation when LISREL might be used, imagine an attrition study similar to the one discused in the earlier path analysis section of this chapter, with the exception that now the study is designed to test a slightly different model of student attrition. The previous model included only academic types of variables. In this LISREL example, the model now will include both academic and social integration variables. In this situation, the assumptions are different, and the academic and social integration variables affect each other. Reciprocal causation (a feedback loop) exists in the model, so path analysis is no longer appropriate. LISREL must now be used to estimate the parameters of the model and to indicate the net effect of both academic integration on social integration and also social integration on academic integration. Examples of LISREL as a research tool are found in Terenzini and Wright (1987), and Voorhees (1985).

LISREL is a complex methodology, and this chapter provides only a brief introduction. Informative discussions on LISREL can be found in Duncan (1966), Kerlinger (1986), Pedhazur (1982), and Wolfle (1977, 1980, and 1985).

Causal Modeling as an Institutional Research Tool

The first step in any research is to determine the question that must be answered and then to assess which technique is the most useful. The kinds of questions for which causal modeling may be useful involve the relationships of a number of independent variables to a single dependent variable, when controling for all the other variables in the model is desirable. Causal modeling assesses changes in student behavior, attitudes, motivation, and ability and determines the impact of various programs on student outcomes. In situations when subjects are measured at several points in time on the same variable (for example, GPA collected for each quarter in school), causal modeling is especially useful.

The computer is essential to causal modeling; the numerous equations are too tedious to be calculated by hand. The calculations for a path analysis may be done with whatever computer package is preferred by or available to the researcher. The multivariate statistical procedures and packaged computer programs such as the Statistical Package for the Social Sciences (SPSS; a registered trademark of SPSS, Inc., 444 N. Michigan Ave., Chicago, Ill. 60611), the Statistical Analysis System (SAS; a registered trademark of SAS Institute, Inc., Box 8000, Cary, N.C. 27511-8000), and BMDP (a registered trademark of BMDP Statistical Software, 1964 Westwood Blvd., Ste. 202, Los Angeles, CA 90025) statistical software can be used to assess the fit of the model to the data. The use of LISREL requires that a version of LISREL software be available on the computing system. There have been numerous updates since the original LISREL, the most current version being LISREL VI. Jöreskog very recently completed work on LISREL VII, which runs on a personal computer—a move that may encourage even more researchers to consider causal modeling.

A researcher who wants to make the transition from least squares regression to maximum-likelihood method might begin by analyzing a simple, single-indicator, recursive model with the least squares method and then reanalyze that same model with LISREL. After that experience, it should become more comfortable to use LISREL in the analysis of nonrecursive, multiple-indicator, and more complex models.

The results of the causal modeling analysis should be presented in forms other than regression equations or the original computer output. Two ways that the information might be presented are through crosstabs or graphical presentations. Crosstabs with only two or three categories could be constructed to present the frequencies and percentages for the particular set of variables of interest to the administrator. Another method is to use graphics to portray the important findings. A series of line graphs can be presented to display the linear relationships between pairs of important variables. A circle or pie chart, in which the total pie represents 100 percent of the variance in the dependent variable, can display the proportion of variance explained by the total causal model. Another version of a pie chart, divided to show the portion of variance attributable to each of the variables in the model, could represent the amount of variance explained by the causal model. Available computer graphics packages transform numerical data into various graphical forms that represent the data. Graphics are a very useful, simple, and straightforward way of presenting information. For further discussion of graphics, readers are directed to Mims, 1987.

Implications for Institutional Researchers

Institutional researchers must become familiar with causal modeling methodologies, so they will know when they can benefit from these methodologies. Researchers also need to know about causal modeling techniques and assumptions in order to adequately evaluate the numerous causal modeling studies now being published. Causal modeling, a fad with application to many areas, frequently is applied with little regard for the assumptions. When researchers examine causal modeling studies, they need to evaluate whether they want to accept, reject, or at the minimum question the obtained results.

Some researchers consider that the use of causal data analysis by social scientists can and should be increased, believing that the future will witness a decrease in the use of frequency and percentage crosstabs relative to the total body of research. Asher (1983) states that in light of the "move toward greater sophistication in data analysis techniques, a solid foundation in and understanding of the basic regression model along with an awareness of the properties of various estimation techniques would suffice to expand the analytic horizons of most social scientists" (p. 82).

Asher (1983) also concludes that little attempt is being made to present the causal modeling techniques in language that more people can understand and exploit; therefore, there is "a gap between what can be done in data analysis and what is actually being done" (p. 82). This chapter presents an introduction to causal modeling that will encourage institutional researchers to fill that gap.

References

Anderson, J. G. "Causal Models in Educational Research: Nonrecursive Models." *American Educational Research Journal*, 1978, *15*, 81–97.

Asher, H. B. *Causal Modeling.* (2nd ed.) Newbury Park, Calif.: Sage, 1983.

Bentler, P. M., and Weeks, D. G. "Linear Structural Equations with Latent Variables." *Psychometrika*, 1980, *45*, 289–308.

Blalock, H. M., Jr. (ed.). *Causal Models in the Social Sciences.* Hawthorne, Ill.: Aldine, 1971.

Blalock, H. M., Jr. *Social Statistics.* (2nd ed.) New York: McGraw-Hill, 1972.

Duncan, O. D. "Path Analysis: Sociological Examples." *The American Journal of Sociology*, 1966, *72* (1), 1–16.

Duncan, O. D. *Introduction to Structural Equation Models.* Orlando, Fla.: Academic Press, 1975.

Jöreskog, K. G. "A General Method for Estimating a Linear Structural Equation System." In A. S. Goldberger and O. D. Duncan (eds.), *Structural Equation Models in the Social Sciences.* New York: Seminar Press, 1973.

Jöreskog, K. G., and Sörbom, D. "LISREL IV: Analysis of Linear Structural Relationships by the Method of Maximum Likelihood." Chicago: National Educational Resources, 1978.

Jöreskog, K. G., and Sörbom, D. "LISREL VI: Analysis of Linear Structural Relationships by Maximum Likelihood and Least Squares Methods." Chicago: National Educational Resources, 1983.

Kenny, D. A. *Correlation and Causality.* New York: Wiley, 1979.

Kerlinger, F. N. *Foundations of Behavioral Research.* (3rd ed.) New York: Holt, Rinehart & Winston, 1986.

Land, K. C. "Principles of Path Analysis." In E. F. Borgatta (ed.), *Sociological Methodology.* San Francisco: Jossey-Bass, 1969.

76

Loether, H. J., and McTavish, D. G. *Descriptive and Inferential Statistics.* (2nd ed.) Newton: Allyn & Bacon, 1980.

Long, J. S. *Covariance Structure Models: An Introduction to LISREL.* Newbury Park, Calif.: Sage, 1983.

Mims, R. S. (ed.). *The Design, Production, and Use of Computer Graphics: A Tutorial and Resource Guide.* Tallahassee, Fla.: The Association for Institutional Research, 1987.

Moline, A. E. "Financial Aid and Student Persistence: An Application of Causal Modeling." *Research in Higher Education,* 1987, *26* (2), 130–147.

Norušis, M. J. *SPSS-X, Advanced Statistics Guide.* New York: McGraw-Hill, 1985.

Pascarella, E. T., and Terenzini, P. T. "Predicting Voluntary Freshman Year Persistence/Withdrawal Behavior in a Residential University: A Path Analytic Validation of Tinto's Model." *Journal of Educational Psychology,* 1983, *75,* 215–226.

Pedhazur, E. J. *Multiple Regression in Behavioral Research.* (2nd ed.) New York: Holt, Rinehart & Winston, 1982.

Terenzini, P. T., and Wright, T. M. "Influences on Students' Academic Growth during Four Years of College." *Research in Higher Education,* 1987, *26* (2), 161–179.

Tinto, V. "Dropout from Higher Education: A Theoretical Synthesis of Recent Research." *Review of Educational Research,* 1975, *45,* 89–125.

Voorhees, R. A. "Student Finances and Campus-Based Financial Aid: A Structural Model Analysis of the Persistence of High Need Freshman." *Research in Higher Education,* 1985, *22,* 65–92.

Wolfle, L. M. "An Introduction to Path Analysis." *Multiple Linear Regression Viewpoints,* 1977, *8,* 36–61.

Wolfle, L. M. "Strategies of Path Analysis." *American Educational Research Journal,* 1980, *17* (2), 183–209.

Wolfle, L. M. "Applications of Causal Models in Higher Education." In J. Smart (ed.), *Higher Education: Handbook of Theory and Research.* Vol. 1. New York: Agathon Press, 1985.

Wright, S. "Correlation and Causation." *Journal of Agricultural Research,* 1921, *20,* 557–585.

Wright, S. "The Method of Path Coefficients." *Annals of Mathematical Statistics,* 1934, *5,* 161–215.

Arlett E. Moline is a consultant in educational psychology and institutional research. Formerly, she was assistant to the director of the Education Planning and Development Office at the University of Minnesota, where she completed her doctorate in educational psychology. Her interests include the study of financial aid and student persistence in higher education, causal modeling, and the development of computer data bases.

Increasing demand for accurate forecasts in such areas as
student enrollment, energy expenditures, and facility capacity
are placing new demands on the institutional researcher.

Forecasting Methods
for Institutional Research

Linda W. Jennings, Dean M. Young

The need for institutions to develop long-range goals and planning places
an increased premium on accurate forecasts. Colleges, universities, and
other institutions are becoming more aware of the demand for forecasting
such quantities as tuition costs, student enrollment, and faculty salaries in
order to plan for adequate facilities and revenues in the coming years.
The necessity for improved accuracy has placed increased importance on
the methods used to implement these forecasts. Although many new forecasting methodologies are currently available, few are actually applied
because of the degree of statistical literacy needed to apply these methods.
The purpose of this chapter is to give a brief review of the current forecasting methods and an overview and example of one of the more accurate
methodologies—times series analysis using the *Box-Jenkins method.*

Taxonomy of Forecasting Methods

In reviewing the forecasting literature, we shall use the taxonomy
developed by Nelson (1973), who classifies forecasting methods into five
basic categories: *subjective methods, ad hoc methods, structural equation
methods, deterministic model methods,* and *time series analysis methods.*
We shall first give a brief overview of each forecasting methodology.

B. D. Yancey (ed.). *Applying Statistics in Institutional Research.*
New Directions for Institutional Research, no. 58. San Francisco: Jossey-Bass, Summer 1988.

Subjective Forecasting Methods. Probably the most widely applied methodology is forecasting based on experience and intuition. Many institutional officers and planners are quite willing to use subjective forecasts. Several reasons for this phenomenon are the following: This is the only method in which they are experienced, forecasts using this method have been reasonably accurate, and the scope and complexity of the problems are so large that other approaches would be prohibitive.

However, this method of forecasting has several drawbacks. The accuracy may vary widely from individual to individual. One way of adjusting for the variability in individual forecasts is to combine subjective probabilities. Using this technique, the forecaster selects a forecast value deemed most likely to occur and gives a subjective probability that this value will be exceeded. The forecasts may be combined using one of several different methods. A review of methods for combining subjective probabilities is given in Genest and Zidek (1986).

Ad Hoc Forecasting Methods. Most of these forecasting methods are intuitive rules of thumb for combining previous observations collected over time. This set of observations is generally referred to as a *time series*. One commonly applied technique is the moving average forecasting method. In this technique a forecast is made by averaging the observations from the previous k time periods. However, this method has a tendency to overestimate or underestimate the true value when the time series is either steadily increasing or steadily decreasing.

A second widely applied ad hoc forecasting tool is the exponential smoothing method. For this method the estimate of the forecasted variable is a weighted combination of the actual and forecasted value of the current time period. The weight assigned to the actual value for the current period, which is a value between 0 and 1, is known as the "smoothing constant." Given that F is the forecasted value, A is the actual observation, and α is the smoothing constant, the forecasted value may be expressed as

$$F_{t+1} = \alpha A_t + (1 - \alpha)_t.$$

The name of the procedure is derived from the exponentially decreasing weight placed on the historical observations. When the weight value is $\alpha = 2/(N + 1)$, exponential smoothing is equivalent to the moving average method, in which N is the number of observations used in calculating the moving average.

Double exponential smoothing is an ad hoc forecasting technique that extends the single exponential smoothing method to allow for the effect of a trend. The double exponential smoothing forecasted value may be expressed as

$$F_{t+1} = 2g_1(t) - g_2(t - 1),$$

where F is the forecasted value, g_1 is the single smoothed forecast for period t, and $g_2(t - 1)$ is the double function value for period $t - 1$ given by

$$g_2(t - 1) = \alpha g_1(t) + (1 - \alpha)g_2(t - 1).$$

Another ad hoc forecasting method is the Holt-Winters method developed by Holt (1957) and Winters (1960). In this method a nonseasonal time series, that is, a time series which assumes no repeating periodic fluctuation, is considered to be composed of a trend and a level. This method is similar to the approach taken in double exponential smoothing; however, the double exponential smoothing formula is not applied. The trend values are directly smoothed, allowing more flexibility, since the trend can be smoothed with a different parameter from the one used in the original series. This method can also forecast seasonal time series via a slight modification.

Structural and Econometric Models. Structural models are sets of mathematical equations that represent causal relationships among factors affecting the dependent variable. These models range from a single regression model to a set of simultaneous equation models. Structural equation models are typically used to describe relationships among an interdependent system of endogenous (dependent) variables as a function of exogenous (independent) variables. The most difficult problems associated with the formulation of structural equation models are that many constructs are not directly measurable and that variables contain a large amount of measurement error.

Jöreskog (1973) has developed a general linear structural equation model, known as LISREL, that formulates models with latent variables, measurement error, and reciprocal causation (see Chapter Five). The LISREL model consists of two segments: the measurement model and the structural equation model. The measurement model describes the relationships between latent variables and the observed variables, whereas the structural equation model specifies the causal relationships among the latent variables. Detailed discussions concerning modeling with LISREL can be found in Jöreskog and Sörbom (1978), and a detailed discussion concerning structural equation models may be found in Jöreskog and Sörbom (1979). Procedures for estimating simultaneous equation models are described in Pindyck and Rubinfeld (1976) and Kmenta (1971).

Deterministic Models. An alternative approach, univariate time series analysis, involves the decomposition of the time series into four components: trend, seasonal variation, cyclic variation, and irregular variation, as discussed by Harnett (1970). The trend component represents the long-term movement of the series. Seasonal variation accounts for periodic behavior, and cyclic variation represents patterns repeated over time at varying intervals. Business cycles are the most frequently cited examples of cyclic variation. Irregular variation represents unpredictable variation or random error.

Wold (1954) provided a theoretical basis for deterministic models by showing that any time series with a constant mean, called a stationary time series, can be decomposed into a purely deterministic component and a purely nondeterministic component. The reader is referred to this reference for a more detailed discussion.

Time Series Analysis. Of the five forecasting methodologies, the most rigorously defensible method is time series analysis. The unique characteristics of time series analysis are that the sequence of observations, $z_1, ..., z_n$, is viewed as a realization of a stochastic process of jointly distributed random variables and that conditional probability statements about future observations can be made from the knowledge of the distribution and prior observations. However, the underlying process is generally inferred solely from the historical observations.

Two basic approaches to time series analysis exist: the spectral domain approach and the time domain approach. Spectral analysis views a time series as a complex wave pattern composed of a weighted sum of sine and cosine components. The most common form of time domain time series analysis is the Box-Jenkins time series analysis. We shall concentrate in this forecasting discussion on applications of the Box-Jenkins models. A complete discussion of Box-Jenkins time series analysis can be found in Box and Jenkins (1970) or Granger and Newbold (1977). Portions of the following discussion are taken from Thrasher (1980).

Box-Jenkins Forecasting Methodology

Box-Jenkins analysis represents a time series as a finite linear combination of prior observations and random errors. The time series is assumed to have the same mean for all time periods. This property is known as stationarity. If this condition is not met, then it is assumed that stationarity can be induced by differencing the observations. Differencing a time series simply amounts to subtracting the first observation from the second, the second from the third, and so on. If the stationarity does not disappear, then the procedure is applied to the values obtained after the first differencing to produce second differences.

To be more specific, define the backwards operator B by

$$BZ_t = Z_{t-1}.$$

Applying B to an observation yields the observation from the preceding time period. Differencing of degree d is accomplished by applying the polynomial operator $(1 - B)^d$ on the time series of interest.

For stationary time series, the standard Box-Jenkins model is symbolically expressed as

$$Z_t = \phi_1 Z_{t-1} + \phi_p Z_{t-p} + \theta_0 + \epsilon_1 + \theta_1 \epsilon_{t-1} - \ldots - \theta^q \epsilon_{t-q}. \tag{1}$$

The coefficients $\phi_1, \ldots, \phi_p$ are called autoregressive parameters, and the coefficients $\theta_1, \ldots, \theta_q$ are called moving average parameters. The random errors ϵ_{t6} are assumed to be independent and normally distributed with mean zero and common variance σ_ϵ. The location parameter θ_0 is generally set to zero by subtracting the mean from each random variable in the time series. By defining the autoregressive and moving average operators by

$$\phi(B) = 1 - \phi_1 B - \ldots - \phi_p B^p$$

and

$$\theta(B) = 1 - \theta_1 B - \ldots - \theta^q B^q,$$

respectively, the Box-Jenkins autoregressive integrated moving average (ARIMA) model with degree of differencing d may be expressed as

$$\phi(B) (1 - B)^d Z_t = \theta_0 + \theta(B)\epsilon_t.$$

The term *integrated* refers to the successive summation necessary to remove the differencing. The time series literature refers to these models as ARIMA (p,d,q) models where p is the order of the autoregressive term, q is the order of the moving average term, and d is the order of differencing. For seasonal time series, Box and Jenkins (1970) suggest a multiplicative model of the form

$$\phi'(B^s) \phi(B) (1 - B^s)^d (1 - B)^d Z_t = \theta'(B^s)\theta(B)\epsilon_t,$$

where s is the number of seasons, d is the degree of seasonal differencing involved, and the seasonal autoregressive and moving average parameters are defined by

$$\phi'(B^s) = 1 - \phi_1' B^s - \phi_2' B^{2s} - \ldots - \phi'_p B^{Ps}$$

and

$$\theta'(B^s) = 1 - \theta_1' B^s - \theta_2' B^{2s} - \ldots - \theta'^q B^{Qs}.$$

Models such as these are called ARIMA (p,d,q)(P,D,Q)s processes. In this notation, *p, d,* and *q* are defined as above, while *P* is the order of the seasonal autoregressive term, *Q* is the order of the seasonal moving average term, *D* is the order of seasonal differencing, and *s* is the length of the seasonal cycle. From the Box-Jenkins point of view, forecasting the future behavior of any time series entails determining the number of autoregressive and moving average parameters, determining the degree of differencing, estimating the parameters, and using this information and the history of the series to provide a conditional expectation and confidence interval for a given lead time. This is accomplished from an analysis of the data rather than from an a priori assumption about which models might be appropriate. The Box-Jenkins method involves four basic stages: identification, estimation, specification validation, and forecasting. We shall give a brief discussion of each of these four stages.

Identification. The autocorrelation function (ACF), that is, the correlation of the variable we wish to forecast with its own past values, is one of the main diagnostic tools utilized in the identification process. Each ARIMA model is characterized by its autocorrelation function. For example, an ARIMA (0,d,q) process has significant autocorrelation coefficients for the first *q* lags and then vanishes, but an ARIMA (1,d,0) process has an autocorrelation function that decays exponentially. Hence, if we can classify a plot of the autocorrelations as being generated by a particular ARIMA process, we can identify the process generating the time series. Figure 1 depicts the expected autocorrelation functions of several common ARIMA models.

An additional information source for identifying ARIMA processes is the partial autocorrelation function (PACF). Box and Jenkins (1970) have shown that for a purely autoregressive process of order *k*, the autocorrelations $\rho_1, ..., \rho_k$ satisfy the Yule-Walker equations, which can then be solved to provide estimates of the partial autocorrelations. Figure 2 depicts several expected partial autocorrelation functions for some common models.

Nonstationarity reveals itself through the autocorrelation function. For nonstationary processes, the autocorrelation function remains large at large lags. This behavior disappears, however, for appropriately differenced time series data.

In summary, the identification procedure involves inspecting the autocorrelation and partial autocorrelation functions of an empirical time series and its first and second differences. Most time series do not require differencing of degree greater than two.

Estimation. The parameters of an ARIMA process are generally found by minimizing the sum of squared errors

$$S(\phi, \theta) = \sum_{t=0}^{T} \epsilon_t^2$$

Figure 1. Expected Autocorrelation Functions of Some Common
ARIMA Models

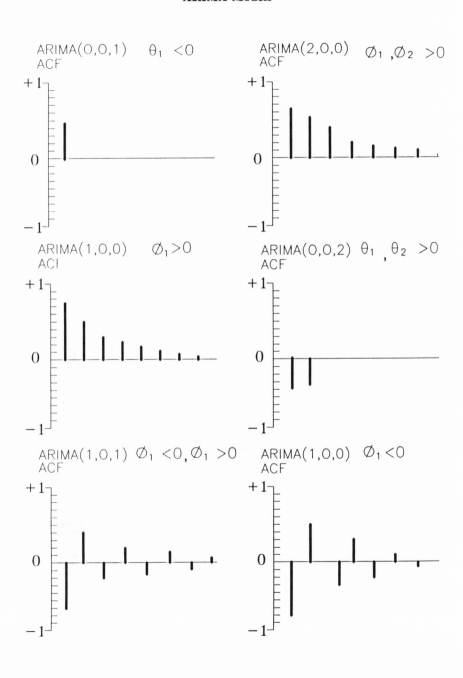

Figure 2. Expected Partial Autocorrelation Functions of Some Common ARIMA Models

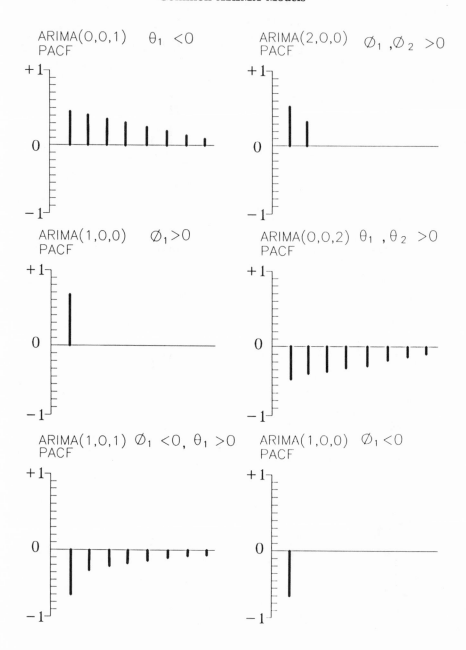

where

$$\epsilon_t = \theta^{-1}(B)\phi(B)W_t \tag{2}$$

and

$$W_t = (1 - B)^d Z_t$$

with Z_t defined as in (1). Since $S(\phi,\theta)$ is nonlinear, estimation of the model parameters is more difficult than in the usual general linear model. A discussion of this estimation algorithm and some of the problems involved in its application can be found in Box and Jenkins (1970).

Application of the ordinary least squares method in conjunction with the linearization process allows approximate standard errors of the coefficients, the multiple correlation coefficient, and other standard statistics to be computed. However, caution should be exercised in interpreting these statistics because the estimation procedure is not the usual least squares algorithm. Approximate standard errors, t statistics, and R^2 values can be calculated from the final iteration.

Diagnosis. Box and Pierce (1970) have shown that the residual autocorrelations are normally distributed random variables with mean 0 and variance $1/T$ for large lags and, hence, that

$$\chi^2(k\text{-}p\text{-}q) = T\sum_{j=1}^{k} \hat{r}_j^2$$

has an approximate chi square distribution with $k - p - g$ degrees of freedom, (T is the number of observations, k is the lag, and r_j is the residual autocorrelation with lag k). Utilizing this result, the Box-Pierce test compares the residuals for a particular model against white noise (a completely random distribution with a mean of zero and a finite variance). If no statistically significant difference is found, a suitable model has been determined).

Thus, application of the Box-Jenkins method of time series estimation proceeds iteratively when we utilize the autocorrelation and partial autocorrelation functions for tentative identification of the underlying stochastic process, estimating the parameters by an iterative linear approximation procedure and testing the residuals against white noise. Several iterations of the identification-estimation-diagnosis sequence may be necessary before a suitable model is determined. Box and Jenkins (1970) have noted that an ARIMA model with as few parameters as possible is preferred.

Forecasting. The goal of the Box-Jenkins procedure is to predict future observations as accurately as possible. One method of defining accuracy is the minimum mean square error criterion, which we shall now define. Let $Z_t(\lambda)$ be the forecasted value λ time periods ahead, based on the empirical observations through time period T. The error may be expressed as

$$e_t(\lambda) = Z^{T+\lambda} - \hat{Z}_t(\lambda),$$

and, therefore, the mean square error that we wish to minimize is

$$E[e_t^2(\lambda)] = E\{[Z_{T+\lambda} - \hat{Z}_t(\lambda)]^2\}.$$

Equation 2 can be employed to re-express a model as an infinite moving average process in the form

$$Z_t = \sum_{j=0}^{\infty} {}_{,j} \epsilon_{t-j} . \tag{3}$$

Since the error terms are independent, it follows that

$$E[e_t^2(\lambda)] = \sigma^\epsilon \sum_{j=0}^{\lambda-1} \Psi_j^2,$$

and, thus, the psi coefficients are a measure of the forecast errors. A practical measure of the forecast accuracy may be gained when we view a plot of the observed values and the forecasted values. Once the point forecast has been established, equation 3 may be used to construct prediction intervals. Forecasts for seasonal series are made in a similar fashion.

Sample Application. The techniques of time series analysis using the Box-Jenkins method will be illustrated with a series of college enrollment data from Baylor University during the period 1960–1985. The analysis was performed using **PROC ARIMA** available in the SAS/ETS (SAS Institute, Inc., 1982) package.

We begin with a time plot of the raw data, which is shown in Figure 3, and examine it for indications of nonstationarity.

In a stationary time series, both the mean and the variance of the series should appear constant over time. There is a steady, nearly linear increase in enrollment over time. The enrollment in the spring semester is consistently lower than that of the preceding fall semester. The data appear to have a seasonal pattern with $s = 2$. The ACF and PACF in Figure 4 provide additional evidence that differencing of the series is required. The ACF remains large for large lags. Since the ACF indicates that the series is nonstationary, no additional information is provided by the PACF.

Figure 3. Plot of Original Data: Annual Enrollment by Semester from 1960–1985

```
  T        X     MIN                                                    MAX
                 4658                                                 11360
                 *-----------------------------------------------------*
  1      4994    |    X                    |                            |
  2      4658    |X                        |                            |
  3      5187    |      X                  |                            |
  4      4965    |   X                     |                            |
  5      5409    |         X               |                            |
  6      5144    |       X                 |                            |
  7      5879    |              X          |                            |
  8      5478    |          X              |                            |
  9      5946    |             X           |                            |
 10      5668    |           X             |                            |
 11      6156    |               X         |                            |
 12      5826    |            X            |                            |
 13      6401    |                X        |                            |
 14      6010    |             X           |                            |
 15      6645    |                 X       |                            |
 16      6270    |              X          |                            |
 17      6471    |               X         |                            |
 18      6210    |              X          |                            |
 19      6440    |               X         |                            |
 20      6123    |              X          |                            |
 91      7051    |                   X     |                            |
 22      6576    |                 X       |                            |
 23      7607    |                    X    |                            |
 24      7210    |                  X    | |                            |
 25      8105    |                       | X                            |
 26      7688    |                     X| |                             |
 27      8322    |                       |  X                           |
 28      7959    |                       |X                             |
 29      8628    |                       |    X                         |
 30      8247    |                       | X                            |
 31      8947    |                       |      X                       |
 32      8550    |                       |    X                         |
 33      9322    |                       |        X                     |
 34      8690    |                       |     X                        |
 35      9386    |                       |        X                     |
 36      8884    |                       |      X                       |
 37      9594    |                       |         X                    |
 38      9131    |                       |       X                      |
 39      9991    |                       |           X                  |
 40      9414    |                       |        X                     |
 41     10263    |                       |            X                 |
 42      9682    |                       |          X                   |
 43     10320    |                       |             X                |
 44      9766    |                       |          X                   |
 45     10666    |                       |              X               |
 46     10088    |                       |           X                  |
 47     10840    |                       |              X             | |
 48     10224    |                       |            X                 |
 49     11360    |                       |                        X|    |
 50     10603    |                       |                     X      |  |
                 *-----------------------------------------------------*
```

Figure 4. Model Identification Using Undifferenced Data: Annual Enrollment by Semester from 1960–1985

ARIMA PROCEDURE

```
LAG COVARIANCE CORRELATION -1 9 8 7 6 5 4 3 2 1 0 1 2 3 4 5 6 7 8 9 1
  0   3610895    1.00000   |                        |********************|
  1   3277113    0.90756   |                     .  |******************  |
  2   3182336    0.88131   |                     .  |******************  |
  3   2865619    0.79360   |                   .    |***************     |
  4   2778358    0.76944   |                  .     |***************     |
  5   2462845    0.68206   |                .       |*************.      |
  6   2366018    0.65524   |               .        |*************  .    |
  7   2082866    0.57683   |               .        |************   .    |
  8   1997556    0.55320   |              .         |***********     .   |
  9   1701222    0.47114   |            .           |*********        .  |
 10   1598751    0.44276   |           .            |*********        .  |
```

'.' MARKS TWO STANDARD ERRORS

PARTIAL AUTOCORRELATIONS

```
LAG CORRELATION -1 9 8 7 6 5 4 3 2 1 0 1 2 3 4 5 6 7 8 9 1
  1    0.90756   |                    .   |******************  |
  2    0.32692   |                    .   |*******             |
  3   -0.26325   |                  .*****|        .           |
  4    0.17350   |                    .   |***     .           |
  5   -0.19781   |                  . ****|        .           |
  6    0.09077   |                    .   |**      .           |
  7   -0.08049   |                    . **|        .           |
  8    0.04626   |                    .   |*       .           |
  9   -0.13413   |                    . ***|       .           |
 10    0.01988   |                    .   |        .           |
```

AUTOCORRELATION CHECK FOR WHITE NOISE

```
TO    CHI                       AUTOCORRELATIONS
LAG  SQUARE DF   PROB
 6   206.33  6  0.000   0.908  0.881  0.794  0.769  0.682  0.
```

If the seasonal pattern in the data had not been so apparent, as demonstrated by the clear differences in enrollment for spring and fall semesters, the next step might have been to perform a nonseasonal first differencing of the data ($d = 1$).

An examination of the original series reveals that the ACF drops off very slowly to zero. We need to compute the differences $Z_t = X_t - X_{t-2}$, that is, difference once ($D = 1$) with a seasonal length of 2 ($s = 2$). Figure 5 shows the resulting ACF and PACF for this series. The ACF for the seasonally differenced series suggests that the series is now stationary.

We now begin to select tentative models. The layout in Figure 6 shows the patterns we can expect to find in the ACF and PACF for selected models. ARIMA(p,d,q)(P,D,Q)s models, which have both regular and seasonal components, have interaction terms, so we must examine the entire ACF and PACF. Generally, regular and seasonal factors are of the same type, either autoregressive or moving average.

Figure 5. Model Identification Using Seasonally Differenced Data: Annual Enrollment by Semester from 1960-1985

ARIMA PROCEDURE

AUTOCORRELATIONS

```
LAG COVARIANCE CORRELATION -1 9 8 7 6 5 4 3 2 1 0 1 2 3 4 5 6 7 8 9 1
  0   29247.6    1.00000   |                     |********************|
  1   13607.6    0.46526   |                  .  |********            |
  2    5591.36   0.19117   |                  .  |****    .           |
  3    3397.52   0.11616   |                  .  |**      .           |
  4   -5775.2   -0.19746   |             .  ****|        .           |
  5   -5664.8   -0.19368   |             .  ****|        .           |
  6   -6824.4   -0.23333   |             . *****|        .           |
  7   -3336.7   -0.11408   |                .  **|       .           |
  8    1567.72   0.05360   |                  . |*       .           |
  9    -708     -0.02421   |                  . |        .           |
 10   -2694.2   -0.09212   |                  .  **|     .           |
```
'.' MARKS TWO STANDARD ERRORS

PARTIAL AUTOCORRELATIONS

```
LAG CORRELATION -1 9 8 7 6 5 4 3 2 1 0 1 2 3 4 5 6 7 8 9 1
  1   0.46526   |                 .  |********            |
  2  -0.03228   |                 .  *|       .           |
  3   0.05029   |                 .  |*      .           |
  4  -0.34076   |           *******|         .           |
  5   0.04518   |                 . |*       .           |
  6  -0.18504   |              . ****|        .           |
  7   0.19942   |                 . |****     .           |
  8  -0.00370   |                 . |        .           |
  9  -0.07795   |                 . **|       .           |
```

AUTOCORRELATION CHECK FOR WHITE NOISE

```
 TO    CHI               AUTOCORRELATIONS
LAG  SQUARE DF   PROB
 6   21.01   6  0.002  0.465  0.191  0.116 -0.197 -0.194 -0.233
```

Figure 6. ACF and PACF Patterns for Selected Models

Model	ACF	PACF
Moving Average ARIMA(0,0,q)	Spikes at first q lags, followed by zeroes	decays exponentially
Seasonal Moving Average ARIMA(0,0,Q)s	Q spikes at first Q seasonal lags followed by zeroes	decays from seasonal lag to seasonal lag
Autoregressive ARIMA(p,0,0)	decays exponentially	spikes at first p lags followed by zeroes
Seasonal Autoregressive ARIMA(P,0,0)s	decays from seasonal lag to seasonal lag	P spikes at first P seasonal lags followed by zeroes
Mixed Autoregressive Moving Moving Average ARIMA(p,d,q)(P<D<Q)s	decays exponentially	decays exponentially

Patterns evident in the ACF and PACF guide the model selection process. However, the patterns seen in the sample ACF and PACF can deviate from the theoretical patterns of the underlying process, especially for relatively short series. For many series that occur in the social sciences, models with values for p, q, P, and Q of 0,1, or sometimes 2 frequently prove to be adequate. It is best to begin with simple models, assess the effect on the residuals, and expand the model based on these results.

The ACF for the enrollment data has one significant spike at lag 1. Other nonsignificant but relatively high spikes appear at lags 2,4,5, and 6. For the PACF, significant spikes occur at lags 1 and 4, and moderately large nonsignificant spikes occur at lags 6 and 7. Since the ACF has only one significant lag, the first model estimated was an ARIMA(0,0,1)(0,1,0)2. This model failed to converge. Looking more closely at the ACF, the addition of a seasonal moving average term might be appropriate. The results of the analysis for an ARIMA(0,0,1)(0,1,1)2 model are given in Figure 7. This model appears to give a good fit to the data. The chi square test on the residuals is nonsignificant, and the ACF and PACF for the residuals are both consistent with white noise. Three closely related moving average models; ARIMA(0,0,0)(0,1,1)2; ARIMA(0,0,2)(0,1,0)2; and ARIMA(0,0,0)(0,1,2)2 were also estimated, but provided no improvement in fit.

The pattern of spikes in the PACF in Figure 4 indicates that the series might also be successfully modeled by an autoregressive process. The best fit is provided by the ARIMA(1,0,0)(0,1,0)2 model given in Figure 8. Three models that add an additional parameter to the ARIMA (1,0,0)(0,1,0)2 were also considered. However, no improvement resulted from the ARIMA(2,0,0)(0,1,0)2, ARIMA(1,0,0)(1,0,0)2, or ARIMA(1,0,0) (0,1,0)2 models.

A final choice must be selected from the tentative models. Noting the previous discussion, the ARIMA(0,0,1)(0,1,1)2 model seems to be the best moving average model, and the ARIMA(1,0,0)(0,1,0)2 is the best autoregressive model. Reviewing the diagnostic information, both models have nonsignificant chi square tests for the residual ACFs. The residual ACF and PACF plots for each seem consistent with white noise, although higher spikes remain for the autoregressive model. The standard error estimates for each model are nearly the same. Residual plots for each are also similar. The autoregressive model includes one less parameter to estimate and so might be preferred on the basis of parsimony. The models seem essentially equivalent, and either could be used. However, since the goal of the analysis is to construct a model for forecasting, our final decision on model selection should be based on which gives the best forecasts.

Plots of the original series, forecasted values, and lower and upper 95 percent confidence limits are given for the ARIMA(1,0,0)(0,1,0)2 and ARIMA(0,0,1)(0,1,1)2 models in Figures 9 and 10, respectively.

Figure 7. Estimation for ARIMA(0,0,1)(0,1,1)2 Model: Annual Enrollment by Semester from 1960–1985

```
ARIMA: CONDITIONAL LEAST SQUARES ESTIMATION

                                 APPROX.
        PARAMETER    ESTIMATE   STD ERROR   T RATIO  LAG
        MU            -3.0977    49.7479     -0.06    0
        MA1,1        -0.796278    0.116785   -6.82    1
        MA2,1        -0.326674    0.179454   -1.82    2


        VARIANCE  ESTIMATE =    22823.7
        STD ERROR ESTIMATE =    151.075
        NUMBER OF RESIDUALS=       48
        DATA HAVE BEEN CENTERED.
        ESTIMATED MEAN       =   -3.0977
        PERIODS OF DIFFERENCING= 2.
        MOVING AVERAGE FACTORS
                    FACTOR 1: 1+0.796278B**(1)
                    FACTOR 2: 1+0.326674B**(2)


               AUTOCORRELATION CHECK OF RESIDUALS

     TO   CHI                    AUTOCORRELATIONS
     LAG  SQUARE DF   PROB
      6    7.07  3  0.070 -0.212 -0.035  0.165 -0.176  0.015 -0.165
     12    9.31  9  0.409 -0.038  0.145 -0.056  0.017 -0.077 -0.068
     18   12.23 15  0.661 -0.111  0.055 -0.092  0.057  0.097  0.059
     24   16.21 21  0.757 -0.080 -0.046  0.060 -0.142  0.003  0.105


               AUTOCORRELATION PLOT OF RESIDUALS

LAG COVARIANCE CORRELATION -1 9 8 7 6 5 4 3 2 1 0 1 2 3 4 5 6 7 8 9 1
  0    22823.7    1.00000   |                   |*******************|
  1    -4848.3   -0.21242   |             .  ****|        .         |
  2    -803.31   -0.03520   |             .     *|        .         |
  3    3755.71    0.16455   |             .      |***     .         |
  4    -4009.2   -0.17566   |             .  ****|        .         |
  5    341.806    0.01498   |             .      |        .         |
  6    -3769.8   -0.16517   |             .   ***|        .         |
  7    -858.74   -0.03762   |             .     *|        .         |
  8    3299.94    0.14458   |             .      |***     .         |
  9    -1277.3   -0.05597   |             .     *|        .         |
 10    393.223    0.01723   |             .      |        .         |
                         '.' MARKS TWO STANDARD ERRORS


                    PARTIAL AUTOCORRELATIONS
       LAG CORRELATION -1 9 8 7 6 5 4 3 2 1 0 1 2 3 4 5 6 7 8 9 1
         1   -0.21242   |         .  ****|        .               |
         2   -0.08412   |         .    **|        .               |
         3    0.14616   |         .      |***     .               |
         4   -0.11911   |         .    **|        .               |
         5   -0.03503   |         .     *|        .               |
         6   -0.22178   |         .  ****|        .               |
         7   -0.08454   |         .    **|        .               |
         8    0.09905   |         .      |**      .               |
         9    0.04474   |         .      |*       .               |
        10   -0.01905   |         .      |        .               |
```

Figure 8. Estimation for ARIMA(1,0,0)(0,1,0)2 Model: Annual Enrollment by Semester from 1960–1985

ARIMA: CONDITIONAL LEAST SQUARES ESTIMATION

		APPROX.		
PARAMETER	ESTIMATE	STD ERROR	T RATIO	LAG
MU	0.0471383	40.997	0.00	0
AR1,1	0.470284	0.131033	3.59	1

```
VARIANCE  ESTIMATE =   23841.5
STD ERROR ESTIMATE =   154.407
NUMBER OF RESIDUALS=        48
DATA HAVE BEEN CENTERED.
ESTIMATED MEAN         = 0.0471383
PERIODS OF DIFFERENCING= 2.
AUTOREGRESSIVE FACTORS
            FACTOR 1:    1-.470284B**(1)
```

AUTOCORRELATION CHECK OF RESIDUALS

TO LAG	CHI SQUARE	DF	PROB	AUTOCORRELATIONS					
6	7.49	4	0.112	0.010	-0.034	0.181	-0.268	-0.042	-0.170
12	11.10	10	0.350	-0.074	0.156	-0.014	-0.025	-0.067	-0.149
18	14.67	16	0.549	-0.129	0.002	-0.050	0.053	0.142	0.078

AUTOCORRELATION PLOT OF RESIDUALS

```
LAG COVARIANCE CORRELATION -1 9 8 7 6 5 4 3 2 1 0 1 2 3 4 5 6 7 8 9 1
 0    23841.5   1.00000   |                    |********************|
 1     241.24   0.01012   |                  . |                  . |
 2    -818.9   -0.03435   |                  . *|                  . |
 3    4317.28   0.18108   |                  . |****              . |
 4   -6388.6   -0.26796   |             .*****|                  . |
 5     -1006   -0.04219   |                  . *|                  . |
 6   -4064.7   -0.17049   |                  . ***|                . |
 7   -1770.7   -0.07427   |                  . *|                  . |
 8    3725.78   0.15627   |                  . |***               . |
 9    -344.13  -0.01443   |                  . |                  . |
10    -600.95  -0.02521   |                  . *|                  . |
                   '.' MARKS TWO STANDARD ERRORS
```

PARTIAL AUTOCORRELATIONS

```
LAG CORRELATION -1 9 8 7 6 5 4 3 2 1 0 1 2 3 4 5 6 7 8 9 1
 1    0.01012   |                  . |                  . |
 2   -0.03445   |                  . *|                  . |
 3    0.18203   |                  . |****              . |
 4   -0.28384   |             ******|                  . |
 5   -0.00690   |                  . |                  . |
 6   -0.25150   |             .*****|                  . |
 7    0.06088   |                  . |*                 . |
 8    0.06949   |                  . |*                 . |
 9    0.05175   |                  . |*                 . |
10   -0.14106   |                  . ***|                . |
```

Figure 9. ARIMA(1,0,0)(0,1,0)2: Annual Enrollment by Semester from 1960–1985 Forecasting Accuracy Using Seasonally Differenced Data

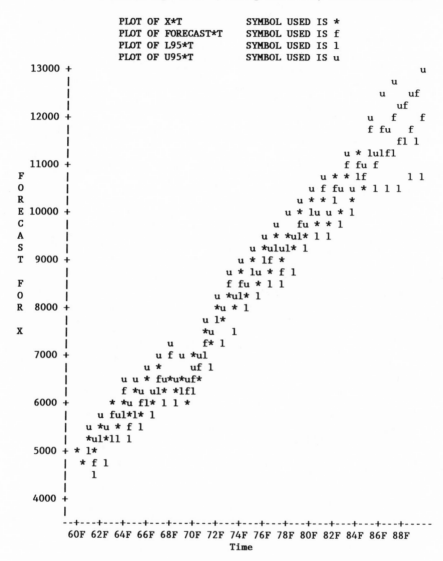

94

Figure 10. ARIMA(0,0,1)(0,1,1)2: Annual Enrollment by Semester from 1960–1985 Forecasting Accuracy Using Seasonally Differenced Data

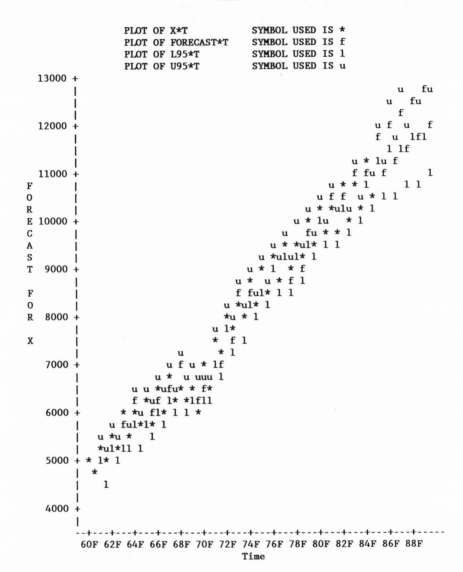

An examination of the two plots shows that the two models perform very similarly in terms of closeness of the actual and forecasted values, width of the confidence interval for predicted values, and tracking the general pattern of the original series. In this case we might select the moving average model, since its seasonal component is consistent with the known seasonal variation of enrollment data.

As with any forecasting model, caution must be exercised when using the Box-Jenkins method to make long-range forecasts. For example, we must assume that the steady upward trend in enrollment for this series will be limited by constraints on the total resources of the university. We must therefore use caution in applying this model for long-range forecasts. A second precautionary note is that the "best fitting" Box-Jenkins model is not necessarily the best forecasting model. It is possible to find an ARIMA model that fits the empirical time series well but produces poor forecasts. The forecaster must keep the criterion of "goodness" in mind when deciding which model to apply to the forecasting problem.

For the novice forecaster who wishes to apply the Box-Jenkins forecasting procedure, we recommend *Applied Time Series Analysis for the Social Sciences* (McCleary and Hay, 1980) and *Time Series and Forecasting: An Applied Approach* (Bowerman and O'Connell, 1979) as excellent references.

Finally, there are now several software packages that provide implementation of the Box-Jenkins forecasting methodology. Among these are SAS, SPSS, and BMDP. The supplement *SAS System for Forecasting Time Series* (Broklebank and Dickey, 1986) is an excellent reference for forecasters using the SAS time series procedures such as PROC ARIMA.

References

Bowerman, B. L., and O'Connell, R. T. *Time Series and Forecasting: An Applied Approach.* N. Scituate, Mass.: Duxbury Press, 1979.

Box, G.E.P., and Jenkins, G. M. *Time Series Analysis: Forecasting and Control.* San Francisco: Holden-Day, 1970.

Box, G.E.P., and Pierce, D. A. "Distribution of Residual Autocorrelations in Autoregressive Integrated Moving Average Time Series Models." *Journal of the American Statistical Association,* 1970, *65,* 1509–1526.

Broklebank, J. C., and Dickey, D. A. *SAS System for Forecasting Time Series.* Cary, N.C.: SAS Institute, Inc., 1986.

Genest, C., and Zidek, J. V. "Combining Probability Distributions: A Critique and an Annotated Bibliography." *Statistical Science,* 1986, *1* (1), 114–148.

Granger, C.W.J., and Newbold, P. *Forecasting Economic Time Series.* New York: Academic Press, 1977.

Harnett, D. L. *Introduction to Satisfied Methods.* Reading, Mass.: Addison-Wesley, 1970.

Holt, C. C. *Forecasting Seasonals and Trends by Exponentially Weighted Moving Averages.* Pittsburgh, Pa.: Carnegie Institute of Technology, 1957.

Jöreskog, K. G. "A General Method for Estimating a Linear Structural Equation System." In A. S. Goldberger and O. D. Duncan (eds.), *Structural Equation Models in the Social Sciences.* New York: Seminar Press, 1973.

Jöreskog, K. G., and Sörbom, D. "LISREL IV Analysis of Linear Structural Relationships by the Method of Maximum Likelihood." User's Guide, Version IV, Rel. 2. Chicago: National Educational Resources, 1978.

Jöreskog, K. G., and Sörbom, D. *Advances in Factor Analysis and Structural Equation Models.* Cambridge, Mass.: Abt Books, 1979.

Kmenta, J. *Elements of Econometrics.* New York: Macmillan, 1971.

McCleary, R., and Hay, R. A. *Applied Time Series Analysis for the Social Sciences.* Newbury Park, Calif.: Sage, 1980.

Nelson, C. R. *Applied Time Series Analysis for Managerial Forecasting.* San Francisco: Holden-Day, 1973.

Newbold, P., and Granger, C.W.J. "Experience with Forecasting Univariate Time Series and the Combination of Forecasts." *Journal of the Royal Statistical Society,* Series A, 1974, *137*, 131–146.

Pindyck, R. S., and Rubinfeld, D. L. *Econometric Models and Economic Forecasts.* New York: McGraw-Hill, 1976.

SAS Institute, Inc. "SAS/ETS." *SAS/ETS User's Guide: Econometrics and Time Series Library.* Cary, N.C.: SAS Institute, Inc., 1982.

Thrasher, G. R. "Box-Jenkins Enrollment Forecasting." Paper presented at the Association for Institutional Research Forum, Atlanta, Ga.: Apr. 1980.

Winters, P. R. "Forecasting Sales by Exponentially Weighted Moving Averages." *Management Science,* 1960, *6*, 324–342.

Wold, H. *A Study in the Analysis of Stationary Time Series.* (2nd ed.) Uppsala, Sweden: Almquist and Wicksell, 1954.

Linda W. Jennings is an assistant professor in Academic Computing Services at the University of Texas Southwestern Medical Center at Dallas in Dallas, Texas.

Dean M. Young is an associate professor of information systems at the Hankamer School of Business, Baylor University, in Waco, Texas.

Testing a hypothesized model is not nearly as difficult as finding the appropriate model to be tested.

Exploratory Data Analysis for Institutional Researchers

Bernard D. Yancey

The statistical methods discussed in previous chapters have been mainly confirmatory in nature, dealing with situations in which hypotheses are being tested. However, what should the institutional researcher do if the primary task is to find an appropriate model rather than to test a hypothesized one? This is a problem particularly when few sound or consistent theories relating to the problem exist or when the number of potential models is large. Earlier chapters have also emphasized the importance of the assumptions underlying the statistical methods. What methods are available to determine whether or not these statistical assumptions have been met?

These questions illustrate the fundamental differences in situations encountered by the institutional researcher and those assumed by the educational researcher, trained primarily in the classical or confirmatory methods. The researcher in the classical approach starts with theory, constructs hypotheses before seeing the data, and then collects and analyzes the data. In contrast, the typical institutional researcher starts with data and data analysis results and then constructs or identifies an appropriate theoretical structure. The institutional researcher is more often describing a given situation rather than testing a theory or set of hypotheses.

B. D. Yancey (ed.). *Applying Statistics in Institutional Research.*
New Directions for Institutional Research, no. 58. San Francisco: Jossey-Bass, Summer 1988.

This chapter demonstrates how *exploratory data analysis* provides an approach that more closely fits situations encountered by institutional researchers and how to use exploratory data analysis effectively in conjunction with confirmatory analysis.

What is Exploratory Data Analysis?

To quote Tukey: "Exploratory data analysis is an attitude, a flexibility, and a reliance on display, NOT a bundle of techniques, and should be taught as so. Confirmatory data analysis, by contrast, is easier to teach and easier to computerize. We need to teach both; to think about science and engineering more broadly; to be prepared to randomize and avoid multiplicity" (1980, p. 23).

The term *confirmatory data analysis* refers to the *classical data analysis* methods as propounded by the Fisher or Pearson-Neyman-Wald schools of thought with emphasis on hypothesis testing, sampling, and significance testing. The many tools and techniques for performing such analyses are thoroughly documented and discussed. Classical methods interpret patterns in data as chance fluctuations using methods that accept rather restrictive underlying statistical assumptions. These particular methods confirm or refute distinct hypothesis constructed prior to seeing the data.

Generally in the classical approach, once the hypothesis has been constructed and the data collected as a random sample or as a sample based on some known probability model, then—depending on the characteristics of the data, the methods used to select the sample, and the hypothesis being tested—a limited number of statistical techniques will yield useful and meaningful results. These characteristics of classical analysis invite cookbook approaches to data analysis. Although these cookbook approaches are attractive to both educators and beginning researchers, they are based on rather restrictive assumptions that may or may not be met. Such techniques are easily applied, but they can produce erroneous results if the underlying statistical assumptions have not been met.

In contrast, while classical data analysis starts with a hypothesis to be tested, exploratory data analysis usually starts with a question that may require a series of analyses. With exploratory data analysis, the researcher searches for the model or models that best describe the structure of the data. The restrictive underlying assumptions with the classical methods primarily allow the researcher to test hypotheses and make statements about statistical significance. With exploratory data analysis considerably fewer underlying assumptions exist.

Although questions may be answered based on the results of exploratory data analysis alone, Tukey (1980) warns that both exploratory and confirmatory analysis are necessary. For example, much exploratory data analysis may be required to determine if the underlying statistical assumptions needed to apply specific classical methods have been met.

The institutional researcher will seldom encounter a situation that exactly matches the ones characterized by the classical approaches. Exploratory data analysis provides an alternative approach and also the means to decide if the data and paradigm meet the requirements of the classical analysis method. A closer look shows that exploratory data analysis is based on four major themes: revelation, re-expression, residuals, and resistance (Hoaglin, Mosteller, and Tukey, 1983).

Revelation. The philosophy underlying exploratory data analysis emphasizes visual displays to reveal the behavior of data, fits, diagnostic measures, and residuals. Graphical displays such as histograms, scattergrams, stem-and-leaf diagrams, and box-and-whisker diagrams explore the data and determine its structure, quantity, and quality. Such displays reveal or suggest relationships among variables, answer questions, and provide useful and critical information for additional analyses.

At the exploratory stage of the analysis, researchers decide if a change of scale (for example, taking natural logs, variance stabilizing transformations) would aid the analysis process. Graphical displays determine whether or not the re-expression of a variable has had the desired effect.

If the analysis includes fitting a model, graphical displays are valuable for examining the residuals.

On a more basic level, graphical displays can identify outliers and other aberrant values.

Re-Expression. Re-expression involves choosing the appropriate scale (for example, logarithmic, square root) to simplify the analysis of the data.

In at least two situations, researchers may consider re-expression. The first is simply when they need a means to interpret and display data. For example, the relationship between two variables, say X and Y, may be easier to see if one of the values is transformed so that the observed relationship is revealed by a scatterplot resembling a straight line rather than some curved function form. In addition, displaying and interpreting data with a wide range of positive values may be easier if the logarithms of the values rather than the raw values are plotted. If two or more batches of data with different scales are being compared, a more legitimate picture of the differences in the distributions of these batches may be obtained if re-expression is used.

A second situation for considering re-expression is when the underlying assumptions required by the statistical analysis procedures are not met. Snedecor and Cochran (1980) discuss re-expression for such failures of assumptions as nonadditivity, heterogeneity of variance and nonnormality, while Box and Cox (1964) discuss a family of power transformations to produce normal-error linear models.

While no strict rules exist for deciding whether or not to re-express a variable when the underlying statistical assumptions have been violated, two brief examples provide a starting point.

When salary data are analyzed, the variance for a particular salary range will likely decrease as mean salary increases. In this situation the variance is clearly not independent of the mean (a violation of the assumption of homogeneity of variance), and applying a logarithmic transformation to the salary variable can stabilize the variance. As a second example, when the data to be analyzed consist of counts, such data are more likely to be *Poisson* (rectangularly distributed) than normally distributed with a variance proportional to the mean. In this situation, taking the square root of the count values can provide a solution to the problem.

Although valuable, re-expression should be used with caution. For instance, when the goal of the analyses is to uncover the underlying structure of the data, then re-expression is extremely useful. If, however, the goal of the analyses is to produce prediction equations applied to future data, re-expression can complicate the situation.

Residuals. One way to understand the underlying structure of a given set of data is to find a model that describes the data. Residuals are the differences between the observed values of a variable and the expected or calculated values based on the model. No data analysis is complete without an examination of the residuals that provides information about the fit and appropriateness of the model. For example, an examination of the residuals plotted against the predicted values reveals not only the degree of fit, but also such violations of assumptions as curvature, non-additivity, and nonconsistancy of variance. Careful examination of the residuals can also help identify outliers and other aberrant observations like miscoded values.

Resistance. Exploratory data analysis emphasizes the methods that are resistant to localized misbehavior in the data. Resistant methods produce estimates of parameters that vary only slightly when small parts of the data are replaced with new values differing dramatically from the original. Resistance should not be confused with robustness, which generally refers to the stability and consistency of the statistic when violations of the underlying statistical assumptions occur.

In estimates of location, for example, the median is a resistant statistic, but not necessarily robust of efficiency. Goodall (1983, p. 349) explains: "An estimator has robustness of efficiency over a range of distributions if its variance (or, for biased estimators, its mean squared error) is close to the minimum for each distribution." In contrast, the arithmetic mean is neither resistant nor robust of efficiency. A variety of statistics, such as the class of M-estimators are resistant and considerably more robust than the median for estimating location. The reader is referred to Goodall (1983, pp. 368–378) for further discussion.

Resistance applies to measures of central tendency such as the median, to the regression techniques discussed by Huber (1981), and to the least median of squares techniques as discussed by Bingen, Siau, and Rousseeuw (1986) and Rousseeuw (1984).

Exploratory Data Analysis and Institutional Research

Of the four major themes of exploratory data analysis—revelation, re-expression, residuals, and resistance—revelation, the cornerstone of the approach, is most worthwhile for the institutional researcher. Revelation, with its heavy dependence on graphical displays, is not only important for exploring data and investigating observed relationships, but also for examining the effects of re-expression, analyzing the residuals, and assessing the resistance of the method.

The remainder of this chapter discusses applying the four themes stressed by exploratory data analysis to problems encountered in institutional research. The section illustrating revelation concentrates on exploring the data and investigating the observed relationships. Illustrations of all four themes are included.

Revelation and Institutional Research. Revelation depends heavily on graphic display. Computer software for graphical display of data provides the institutional researcher with tools for exploring data more easily. Sophisticated graphical software, once limited to powerful and expensive mainframe computers, is now available for microcomputers and is included in statistical packages such as SAS and SPSS-X.

Numerous graphical methods for exploring data exist, but only a few will be discussed here. Du Toit, Steyn, and Stumpf (1986) provide an overview of graphic methods that benefit from statistical software.

Using graphical methods for exploring data is not extraordinary. Some traditional methods such as histograms, pie charts, bar charts, and scatterplots provide useful information, but a new genre of displays directly linked to exploratory data analysis provides more information in a single display.

The traditional histogram produces useful information when the data is categorical as demonstrated in Figure 1, but the 3-D version in Figure 2 is more revealing with the additional dimension. When the data is continuous, however, the traditional histogram can hide important information because the data must be grouped into categories. Figure 3 illustrates distribution of graduate admission grade point averages (ADMGPA) for a group of graduate students. While Figure 3 is informative, much detail is lost. Figure 4 illustrates the use of a stem-and-leaf diagram to display the same data.

Figure 1. Traditional Histogram—Nominal Data

FREQUENCY BAR CHART

RACE		FREQ	CUM. FREQ	PERCENT	CUM. PERCENT
Anglo	`|************************** `	210	210	86.07	86.07
Foreign	`|**`	16	226	6.56	92.62
Minority	`|**`	18	244	7.38	100.00

```
        --------+-------+-------+----
           60      120     180
```

Figure 2. 3-D Histogram—Nominal Data

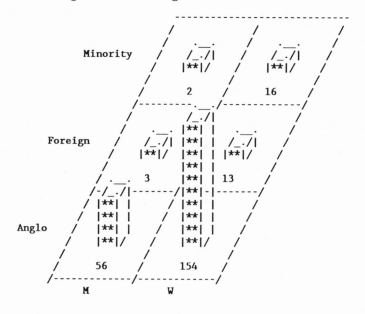

Specifically, Figure 3 shows only that twenty individuals fell into a category with a midpoint of 4.00. Figure 4, however, reveals that seven of these individuals had graduate admission GPAs of 4.00, three had values of 3.90, one had 3.92, two had 3.93, and two had 3.94. Thus, a display that takes up about the same space as the traditional histogram conveys much more information.

When examining continuous data, one goal is to determine the most likely value for a given variable, usually estimated by calculating a measure of central tendency. Depending on the characteristics of the distribution in the population, this value may be the mean, median, or even

Figure 3. Traditional Histogram—Continuous Variables

MIDPOINT ADMGPA		FREQ	CUM. FREQ	PERCENT	CUM. PERCENT
2.25	|**	3	3	1.33	1.33
2.50	|***	6	9	2.67	4.00
2.75	|*****	12	21	5.33	9.33
3.00	|********************	42	63	18.67	28.00
3.25	|**********************	44	107	19.56	47.56
3.50	|*************************	50	157	22.22	69.78
3.75	|************************	48	205	21.33	91.11
4.00	|**********	20	225	8.89	100.00

```
     ----+----+----+----+----+
        10   20   30   40   50
```

FREQUENCY

Figure 4. Stem-and-Leaf Representation—Continuous Data from Figure 3

Variable=ADMGPA

```
Stem Leaf                               #
  40 0000000                            7
  39 00023344                           8
  38 111223333444666788889            21
  37 000123445555669                  15
  36 0001122333344444577777889        24
  35 00001222333456778889             20
  34 1222233344444567888999           22
  33 00134444666778                   14
  32 00000011133455677888999          23
  31 001112233444568                  15
  30 00000000000002333578899          22
  29 0012444577                       10
  28 111234889                         9
  27 278                               3
  26 2556                              4
  25 04                                2
  24 234                               3
  23
  22 7                                 1
  21 39                                2
     ----+----+----+----+----
Multiply Stem.Leaf by 10**-1 (.1)
```

the mode. However, calculating these values is not enough. Also needed is some measure of the accuracy of these estimates, often done by calculating a statistic (usually the standard deviation that provides a numerical representation of the degree of variation). This process leads to a set of statistics that mathematically describes the characteristics of the variable, but whose practical relevance and interpretation are not always obvious. This particular case occurs when a variable such as graduate admission GPA is compared for two or more subgroups, say males and females, within the population. One means of graphically representing such a comparison is box-and-whisker diagrams as illustrated in Figure 5.

Figure 5. Box-and-Whisker Diagram

Schematic Plots

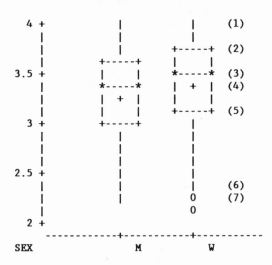

(1) Vertical lines at top of diagram mark values just larger than the 75th percentile (Q3) and the minimum of the maximum value or Q3 plus the QRANGE, where QRANGE – Q3 - Q1, with Q3 and Q1 defined as below.

(2) Q3 – the 75th percentile.

(3) Q2 – the median.

(4) + – the mean.

(5) Q1 – the 25th percentile.

(6) Vertical lines at the bottom of the diagram mark values just smaller than Q1 and the maximum of the minimum value or Q1 - QRANGE.

(7) Values which have approximately a 1 in 20 chance of occurring in a normal distribution.

The box-and-whisker diagram in Figure 5 contains ample information in a small space. Figure 5 indicates the basic differences in the observed distribution of graduate admission GPAs for men and women. For example, the GPAs shifted more toward the higher range for women when compared to the men, and the women have a slightly wider range of GPAs than the men. Both distributions deviate from normality since the rectangles on either side of the median are not equal in size, and the means do not fall on the median line. The rectangle on the high side of the median line being smaller than the one on the low side indicates the distributions are negatively skewed. Such a display is easier to interpret than a summary of the numerical values for the statistics.

Re-Expression and Institutional Research. While re-expression can rescale variables to enhance their graphical display, the technique is most useful when the assumptions of the particular statistical method have been violated. Many violations of assumptions can occur with a large number of additional intervening factors, and no easy or foolproof way exists to detail all the possibilities. However, Snedecor and Cochran (1980), Draper and Smith (1966), Weisberg (1985), and Atkinson (1985) provide discussions and examples of appropriate methods for re-expression or transformation of variables in assorted circumstances to align them with the underlying statistical assumptions.

Nonlinearity is a common problem encountered by institutional researchers when dealing with salary data, linear regression, and heterogeneity of variance. With salary data, the appropriate model may be a nonlinear one of the form $Y = b_0 e^{Xb}$ rather than $Y = b_0 + b_1 X$. If the criterion variable Y is transformed by taking the natural log, then the model becomes $\log Y = \log b_0 + bX$, which is linear. Consider the following series of analyses. The criterion variable is current yearly salary (CURRENT), and the predictor variables are years of service (YRS) and years since Ph.D (YRSPHD).

First, an attempt is made to fit a simple linear model of the form CURRENT = $b_0 + b_1 *$ YRS + $b_2 *$ YRSPHD. The results of this analysis are detailed in Table 1. A plot of the residuals against the predicted values for the model described in Table 1 is shown in Figure 6, which reveals a clear nonlinear trend.

One solution to this problem is to transform either the criterion variable or the predictor variables or both. In this particular situation, the criterion variable, current salary (CURRENT), is transformed by creating a new variable that is the natural log of current salary. Table 2 shows the result of fitting the model with the transformed criterion variable. Not only does this model result in an increase in the R^2 value (from .597 to .645), but an examination of the residuals as seen in Figure 7 reveals a pattern of random residuals about zero, indicating a better fit.

Table 1. General Linear Model
Current Salary = $B_0 + B_1$(Years of Service) + B_2(Years Since Ph.D.) + e
Untransformed Data

General Linear Models Procedure

Dependent Variable: CURRENT

Source	DF	Sum of Squares	Mean Square	F Value	Pr > F
Model	2	2400263024.2	1200131512.1	9.63	0.0027
Error	13	1619350623.8	124565432.6		
Corrected Total	15	4019613648.0			

R-Square	C.V.	Root MSE	CURRENT Mean
0.597138	27.133660	11160.889	41133.000000

Figure 6. Plot of Residuals Against Predicted Values
Current Salary = $B_0 + B_1$(Years of Service) + B_2(Years Since Ph.D.) + e
Untransformed Data

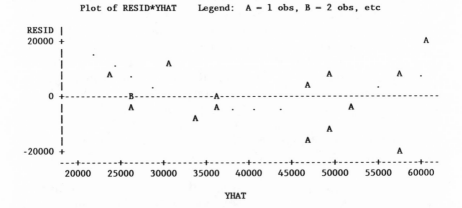

Plot of RESID*YHAT   Legend: A = 1 obs, B = 2 obs, etc

Residuals and Institutional Research. Any statistical analysis that involves fitting a model, whether exploratory or confirmatory, is not complete until the residuals have been examined. The raw residual (RESID) is defined as RESID = OBSERVED – EXPECTED, where OBSERVED is the observed value of a variable and EXPECTED is the predicted value using the model.

One example of the use of residuals was presented in the preceding section. An examination of the residuals assesses the accuracy and appropriateness of a multiple regression model and determines whether or not the underlying assumptions have been met. In addition, an examination of the residuals reveals aberrant data values that indicate data errors.

Table 2. General Linear Model
LN(Current Salary) = B_0 + B_1(Years of Service) + B_2(Years Since Ph.D.) + e
Transformed Data

General Linear Models Procedure

Dependent Variable: LNCUR

Source	DF	Sum of Squares	Mean Square	F Value	Pr > F
Model	2	1.30845164	0.65422582	11.86	0.0012
Error	13	0.71734368	0.05518028		
Corrected Total	15	2.02579533			

R-Square	C.V.	Root MSE	LNCUR Mean
0.645895	2.2248171	0.23490484	10.55838857

Figure 7. Plot of Residuals Against Predicted Values
LN(Current Salary) = B_0 + B_1(Years of Service) + B_2(Years Since Ph.D.) + e
Transformed Data

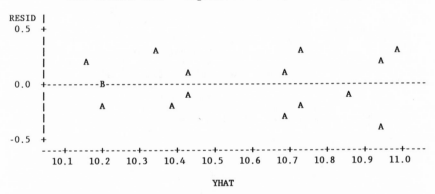

Plot of RESID*YHAT   Legend: A = 1 obs, B = 2 obs, etc.

Ordinary least-squares-based multiple regression is sensitive to outliers; such values have a dramatic impact on the model. The following example demonstrates this fact.

The tested model investigates the relationship between Graduate Record Examinations (GRE) verbal scores, GRE quantitative scores, graduate admission GPAs (GPA in upper division course work), and first year GPA for graduate students in one graduate department. Table 3 reveals the results of the first attempt to fit this model.

An examination of the residuals shown in Figure 8 reveals one aberrant observation. A reexamination of the original data reveals one student almost failed all the first-year courses due to some unusual circumstances.

Table 3. General Linear Model

First Year GPA = B$_0$ + B$_1$(GREV) + B$_2$(GREQ) + B$_3$(Graduate Admission GPA) + e
Full Data Set

General Linear Models Procedure

Dependent Variable: FYGPA

Source	DF	Sum of Squares	Mean Square	F Value	Pr > F
Model	3	3.75439565	1.25146522	7.70	0.0001
Error	207	33.65939713	0.16260578		
Corrected Total	210	37.41379278			

	R-Square	C.V.	Root MSE	FYGPA Mean
	0.100348	11.813797	0.40324407	3.41333175

Figure 8. Plot of Residuals Against Predicted Values

First Year GPA = B$_0$ + B$_1$(GREV) + B$_2$(GREQ) + B$_3$(Graduate Admission GPA) + e
Full Data Set

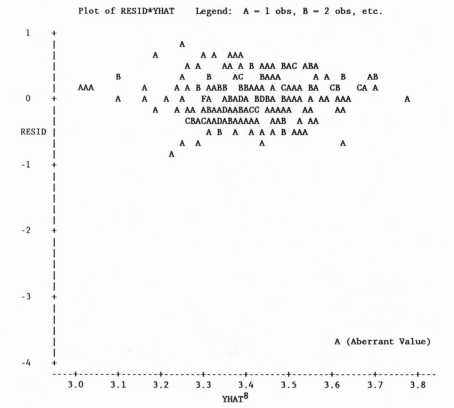

Plot of RESID*YHAT   Legend: A - 1 obs, B - 2 obs, etc.

After the aberrant data point was deleted and the model refitted, the R^2 doubled (from .1003 to .2066) and, more important, there was a 22 percent reduction in the size of the root mean square error (MSE) (from .4032 to .3146), indicating a better fit.

Resistance and Institutional Research. Although there is not sufficient space to discuss more sophisticated methods, a simple example illustrates the concept of resistance.

Table 4 presents data for graduate scholarships awarded in two different departments. If only the mean award is considered, then the departments generally gave the same awards. A review of the medians, however, paints a totally different picture. Fifty percent of the awards in Department X were for $7,350 or more, while 50 percent of the awards for Department Y were only for $4,850 or more. The differences between the awards is more clearly seen in the box-and-whisker diagram provided in Figure 9. Clearly, considering only mean values would have led to some rather misleading conclusions.

Software Packages. The analyses used as examples in this chapter were performed using the person computer (PC) SAS system. Both the

Table 4. Scholarship Awards for Two Graduate Departments

DEPT	X	Y
	$7,500.00	$4,600.00
	$7,600.00	$4,900.00
	$8,000.00	$4,850.00
	$7,350.00	$6,000.00
	$8,000.00	$4,700.00
	$4,200.00	$4,800.00
	$430.00	$4,450.00
	$430.00	$4,900.00
	$430.00	$4,850.00
Mean	$4,882.22	$4,894.44
Median	$7,350.00	$4,850.00

Figure 9. Box-and-Whisker Diagram Data Presented in Table 4

Variable=AWARD

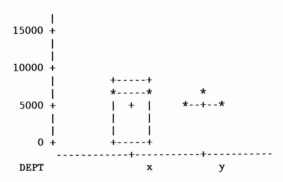

SAS and SPSS-X systems in mainframe and PC versions provide routines for conducting exploratory data analysis. Three other packages for the PC lend themselves to this type of analysis: SYSTAT, Statgraphics (a registered trademark of Statistical Graphics Corp., 2115 East Jefferson St., Rockville, Md. 20852), and GLIM (a project sponsored by the Working party on Statistical Computing of the Royal Statistical Society and developed by R. J. Baker, M.R.B. Clarke, and J. A. Nelder).

In summary, exploratory data analysis is not a set of statistical techniques, but a beneficial approach when applied either alone or in conjunction with confirmatory analysis. The institutional researcher frequently is searching for a model instead of testing a hypothesis; the exploratory data analysis approach produces more immediately meaningful and useful results than do the standard classical approaches.

References

Atkinson, A. C. *Plots, Transformations, and Regression.* Oxford, England: Clarendon Press, 1985.

Bingen, F., Siau, C., and Rousseeuw, P. "Applying Robust Regression Techniques to Institutional Data." *Research in Higher Education,* 1986, *25* (3), 277-297.

Box, G.E.P., and Cox, D. R. "An Analysis of Transformations (with discussion)." *Journal of the Royal Statistical Society,* Series B, 1964, *26,* 211-252.

Draper, N. R., and Smith, H. *Applied Regression Analysis.* New York: Wiley, 1966.

Du Toit, S.H.C., Steyn, A.G.W., and Stumpf, R. H. *Graphical Exploratory Data Analysis.* New York: Springer-Verlag, 1986.

Goodall, C. "M-Estimators of Location: An Outline of the Theory." In D. C. Hoaglin, F. Mosteller, and J. W. Tukey (eds.), *Understanding Robust and Exploratory Data Analysis.* New York: Wiley, 1983.

Hoaglin, D. C., Mosteller, F., and Tukey, J. W. (eds.). *Understanding Robust and Exploratory Data Analysis.* New York: Wiley, 1983.

Huber, P. J. *Robust Statistics.* New York: Wiley, 1981.

Rousseeuw, P. J. "Least Median of Squares Regression." *Journal of the American Statistical Association,* 1984, *77,* 871-880.

Snedecor, G. W., and Cochran, W. G. *Statistical Methods,* (7th ed.) Ames: Iowa State University Press, 1980.

Tukey, J. W. "We Need Both Exploratory and Confirmatory." *The American Statistician,* 1980, *34* (1), 23-25.

Weisberg, S. *Applied Linear Regression.* New York: Wiley, 1985.

Bernard D. Yancey is currently director of institutional research for the University of Colorado at Boulder. He has been a longtime proponent of the use of exploratory data analysis in institutional research.

Index

A

Ad hoc forecasting methods, 77, 78–79
American College Testing Program (ACT), and regression analysis example, 45–49
Analysis of covariance structures, 61
Analysis of variance (ANOVA): assumptions of, 17–18; computers and software for, 20–21; repeating, 19–20; significant versus meaningful differences in, 20; use of, in comparisons, 11–12, 16–21
Anderson, J. G., 61, 75
Applied Time Series Analysis for the Social Sciences, 95
Asher, H. B., 63, 67, 75
Association models, 25, 26–33; and post hoc procedures, 34–35
Atkinson, A. C., 105, 110

B

Bartlett, M. S., 24, 40
Baylor University, in Box-Jenkins application example, 86–95
Belsley, D. A., 50, 55, 60
Bentler, P. M., 72, 75
Bingen, F., 101, 110
Birch, M. W., 23–24, 40
Bishop, Y.M.M., 23–24, 37, 40
Blalock, H. M., 61, 75
BMDP, Inc., 24, 40, 95
Bock, R. D., 23–24, 40
Bowerman, B. L., 49, 60, 95
Box, G.E.P., 80, 82, 85, 95, 99–100, 110
Box-and-whisker diagrams, 104–105; and exploratory data analysis, 99
Box-Jenkins forecasting method, 80–95, 85; diagnosis of, 85; and estimation, 82; and forecasting as goal, 85–86; and identification, 82, 83–84; sample application of, 86–95
Broklebank, J. C., 95
Burke, P. J., 24, 36, 41

C

Campbell, D. T., 5–6, 10
Causal modeling, 61–76; benefits of, 63; causation in, 62; description of, 62–63; history of, 61; implications of, for institutional researchers, 74–75; as institutional research tool, 73–75; and LISREL, 69–73; and path analysis, 64–67; steps for, 63; techniques of, 64
Classical data analysis, 98–99
Classical experimental paradigm, 5–10; data analysis within, 7, 8; elements of, 6; goal of, 6–7; implications for, 8–9; and institutional research situation, 7–8; prerequisites for, 7
Cochran, W. G., 99–100, 105, 110
Comparing groups, using continuous data, 11–22
Computers: and ANOVA, 18–19, 20–21; and exploratory data analysis, 109–110; and t test, 20–21
Confirmatory data analysis, 9–10, 98–99
Continuous data, comparing groups using, 11–22
Cook's D, 49, 50
Cox, D. R., 99–100, 110
Cramer's V, 25

D

Deterministic model forecasting methods, 77, 79–80
Dickey, D. A., 49, 60, 95
Discrimination, testing for, 37–39
Double exponential smoothing, as ad hoc forecasting technique, 78–79
Draper, N. R., 50, 60, 105, 110
Du Toit, S.H.C., 101, 110
Dummy variables, in causal modeling, 68
Duncan, O. D., 61, 63, 73, 75

Lindgren, B. W., 9, 10
Linear structural relations (LISREL), 64, 69-73, 79; advantages and disadvantages of, 72-73; example using, 73; and identification, 72; primary assumption of, 71-72; two major parts of, 71
Littell, R. C., 44, 57, 60
Loether, H. J., 66, 68, 76
Logit models, 25, 33-34; and post hoc procedures, 34-35, 36
Log-linear models, 23-42; and association models, 25, 26-33, 35; hierarchical, for multiple variables, 26-30; and logit models, 25, 27, 33-34, 36; and non-hierarchical analysis, 30-33; and post hoc procedures, 34-35; sampling zeros and structural zeros in, 35-37; strategy for model selection in, 30; and tests for discrimination, 37-39; types of, 25
Long, J. S., 69, 76

M

McCleary, R., 95, 96
McLaughlin, G. W., 25, 26-27, 41
McSweeney, M., 25, 34-35, 41
McTavish, D. G., 66, 68, 76
Mallow's C(P) statistic, 53, 57
Marascuilo, L. A., 25, 34-35, 41
Mendenhall, W., 12, 17, 22
Microstat, 21
Mims, R. S., 74, 76
Moline, A. E., 68-69, 76
Montgomery, D. L., 52, 60
Morrison, D. E., 7, 10
Mosteller, F., 99, 110
Multicollinearity, and regression models, 52, 53
Multiple linear regression models, 52; example and discussion of, 53-57
MULTIQUAL, 24
Myers, R. H., 53, 60

N

Nelson, C. R., 77, 96
Newbold, P., 80, 95, 96
Nonrecursive models, in causal modeling, 64
Noruŝis, M. J., 67, 68, 76

O

O'Connell, R. T., 49, 60, 95

P

Pascarella, E. T., 61, 76
Path analysis, 64-69; advantages and disadvantages of, 68; assumptions of, 65-66; departures from assumptions of, 66-68; example of, 68-69, 70
Pearson, K., 24, 41
Pearson's chi square, 24
Peck, E. A., 52, 60
Pedhazur, E. J., 17, 22, 63, 66, 68, 73, 76
Pierce, D. A., 85, 95
Pindyck, R. S., 79, 96
Post hoc procedures, for log-linear models, 34-35
Preliminary Scholastic Aptitude Test (PSAT), and path analysis example, 69

R

Randomization: and classical experimental paradigm, 6, 8; and t distribution, 14; and t distribution, 13
Recursive models, in causal modeling, 64, 66, 67
Re-expression: and exploratory data analysis, 99-100; and institutional research, 105-106
Regression analysis, 43-60; assumptions in, 45; example and discussion of, 53-57; and influence analysis, 50-52; and least squares, 44-45; and multicollinearity, 53; and multiple linear regression model, 52; and residual analysis, 49-50; and simple linear regression model, 45-49; and variable selection, 52-53
Regression coefficients, 43-44
Residuals: analysis of, in regression models, 49-50, 51; and exploratory data analysis, 100; and institutional research, 106-109
Resistance: and exploratory data analysis, 100-101; and institutional research, 109